2

To Brianna

Best Wishes

from the Author.

Margie Johnson

JOAN OF ARC,
the Heroine

Also by Vargie Johnson

Charles Darwin, the Adventurer
Alexander the Great, the Conqueror
The Autobiography of My Grandfather Tupu

JOAN OF ARC,
the Heroine

Vargie Johnson

Illustrations by Keith Perkins

VANTAGE PRESS
New York

FIRST EDITION

Published by Vantage Press, Inc.
516 West 34th Street, New York, New York 10001

Manufactured in the United States of America
ISBN: 0-533-11720-8

Library of Congress Catalog Card No.: 95-90832

0 9 8 7 6 5 4 3 2 1

To the women who
call me son

With love and respect

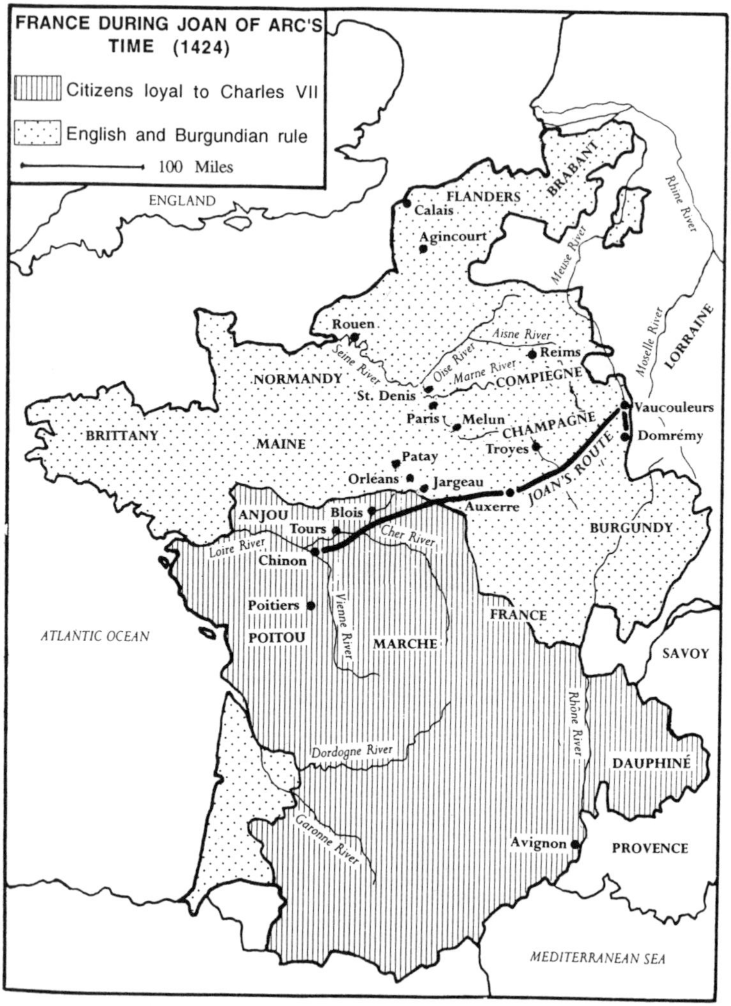
FRANCE DURING JOAN OF ARC'S TIME (1424)
Citizens loyal to Charles VII
English and Burgundian rule
100 Miles
ENGLAND
FLANDERS
BRABANT
Calais
Agincourt
Meuse River
Rhine River
Moselle River
LORRAINE
Rouen
Aisne River
Reims
Seine River
Oise River
Marne River
COMPIEGNE
NORMANDY
St. Denis
Vaucouleurs
Paris
Melun
CHAMPAGNE
Domrémy
BRITTANY
MAINE
Troyes
Patay
JOAN'S ROUTE
Orléans
Jargeau
Auxerre
ANJOU
Blois
Tours
Cher River
BURGUNDY
Loire River
Chinon
Poitiers
Vienne River
FRANCE
ATLANTIC OCEAN
POITOU
MARCHE
SAVOY
Rhône River
Dordogne River
DAUPHINÉ
Garonne River
Avignon
PROVENCE
MEDITERRANEAN SEA

Contents

Acknowledgments

As background reading material the author wishes to acknowledge the following:

- *The Girl in White Armor,* by Albert Bigelow Paine (New York, Macmillan, 1927).
- *Beyond the Myth,* by Polly Schoyer Brooks (New York, J. B. Lippincott, 1990).
- *Joan of Arc,* by Brian Williams (London, Pan Books, 1979).

JOAN OF ARC,
the Heroine

Chapter One
A Hundred Years of War

A prophecy: France would be lost by a woman and saved by a young maiden.

Durand Laxart reporting:

My name is Durand Laxart. You will never have heard of me. To be honest, I am no one special; yet I know a few tales that would make a person's hair curl. In my time I have kept company with many famous people. I have traveled my country far and wide and have witnessed many a battle. Four times I have been close to death and have thought that my time had come. At the height of battle and in the face of the enemy I have seen grown men cry and beg for mercy. Battles against the English and the Burgundians have claimed the lives of some of my closest friends. Life has been hard and tough, yet I am not the sort to complain.

The story I want to tell begins in the year 1412, when a cousin of mine, Joan of Arc, was born.

"Claudine, a messenger has just arrived from Domrémy, from the house of my cousin. Jacques's wife, Isabelle, has just given birth to a baby girl."

"Then you must make haste and ready yourself to leave at once and be among the first to congratulate them. Quickly, send for your horse while there is still enough light in the day to make the journey."

"This is not a good time to bring a young child into the world in Domrémy. That poor village has the misfortune of being located far too close to the Burgundy territory. I hear tell that the raids from Burgundian marauders are becoming more and more frequent."

"Then why don't they leave that area? Durand, invite them back here to stay with us for a while."

"They're a proud lot in Domrémy, Claudine. They won't leave their homes or their land without a good fight."

Yes indeed, Domrémy was not the best of places to be during these times. The people in and around the area had had their fair share of problems with bandits. In fact, much of western France was under English-Burgundian influence and they were causing much havoc among our people. We could see our beloved France slowly slipping away from us as the English acquired more and more land on their conquest east. Unfortunately, at a time when our country needed strong leadership, it wasn't there for us. It was common knowledge far and wide that our king was quite a pathetic character, and more than a few felt that he had gone completely mad. Even Queen Isabelle had given up on him. Many thought that their son Charles, the Dauphin, would make a very weak future king, and he was considered by many a coward also. Oh yes, our country was indeed in big trouble and there were others, other than ourselves, who knew of it, England's young Henry V for one.

"Doesn't anyone live in this house anymore?"

"Durand Laxart, is that you at my door? It is. Please come in. I knew you would not be far behind my messenger. Welcome to Domrémy. Come in and meet our new baby. We've named her Joan."

"Isabelle Romée, she's beautiful. How is it that you and

Jacques always manage to produce such good-looking babies?"

"Thank you, Durand. Pick her up if you wish; she loves to be held. Did you come alone?"

"Yes. Nowadays it's far too dangerous to travel in these parts with the family."

"You're right of course, Durand. Only last week we were raided by the Burgundians again. You may have noticed as you entered our town that several of the buildings have been burned to the ground. Not a pleasant sight."

"When you and the baby are fit and well, you must all come back to Burey with me. It'll be much safer there. Will you come?"

"No, Durand. Our place is here. This is our home and no foreigner is about to drive us away from it. But thank you. You have always been so kind to us."

"So where is the proud father himself? I must toast to his success."

"He's down at the marketplace. There's going to be another burning today. One of the Dupont sisters has been accused of practicing witchcraft, and she is to be burned. This very minute the pyre is being built. People around these parts have been suspicious of her for a long time. Some say that they heard her calling underground spirits yesterday and congratulating them on their success, so they're blaming her for the raiding party that hit us last week. They feel that with her gone, the raids may stop. I'm not so sure. I'm not one to be attending such gatherings, but the people in this town are very excited over the affair. Burnings are becoming more and more frequent around here, and I don't like it. Jacques is there now."

Isabelle was right. Lately the whole of France has seemed to be on a witch-hunt, and like her, I strongly disagree with the practice. Not wanting to experience one at first hand, I made a point of staying well and clear of them. At the moment it doesn't matter where you are in the country; people are always speaking of a trial that is in progress somewhere. I detest the practice and it usually upsets me greatly just being around people discussing one. I know of several women personally who are in prison at the moment awaiting trial. I also know for a fact that they are experiencing appalling conditions. Prisoners who are suspected of witch-craft for the most part are heavily chained so that there is no chance of escape. Their food is of the poorest quality and ill prepared. They are constantly forced to submit to physical examinations of the most debasing kind, in search of any small growth that might answer the description of a witch trait. Some are tortured in a horrific manner while awaiting their trial. I actually think that these poor women long for their trial to begin since it promises an end to the suffering, one way or anther.

The afternoon turned to early evening, and still Jacques was not home. A light wind had started to blow, so I threw a coat over my shoulders and headed toward the center of town to look for him, being fairly confident that at this hour of the day the burning should have been well and truly over. The roads leading toward the marketplace were fairly deserted, and someone had hung colorful banners in the street to announce the day's event.

Once I was at the square, it was a different story. There were people everywhere, milling around in anticipation. I could make out the pyre at the center of the square, and I could see clearly that the faggots had not been struck. Realizing then that the burning had not yet taken place, I turned my back to make a rapid retreat, knowing all too well my strong feelings toward this barbaric practice. But as I turned, madness erupted among the crowd as a series of shouts were heard coming from the direction of the courthouse. People appeared from nowhere, and I was soon surrounded by the bustling masses. I couldn't have escaped even if I'd wanted to and promptly found myself being gradually pushed forward toward the pyre. I could see Miss Dupont being dragged through the angry mob in chains, and they clawed at her as she passed by. My heart went out to her, and I was overcome by grief. I couldn't hold back my tears, and I sobbed loudly like a child being whipped for naughtiness. Because of the noise about me, nobody heard my sobs. Every bone in my body ached for the poor woman.

"Burn the wretch!" shouted angry women from the crowd.

"How dare you live amongst us and dabble in such barbaric rituals!" shouted another. "May God have pity on your soul, you witch!"

"I am not a witch!" came a reply from the Dupont woman as she was being dragged along. "Why are you doing this to me?" But the crowd only laughed at her and mocked her further. Some actually reached out and beat her across the back with sticks as she neared them.

"Maybe we should have hanged her instead. She should suffer a slow death. Maybe the flames are too quick and too good for her." A man's voice could be heard over the noise of the people.

"That'll teach her to worship the devil, provoking our enemy to attack Domrémy," I could hear the woman standing next to me say to her husband. "Maybe her sister is in on this also. Maybe the court master should investigate her as well."

I couldn't stay and listen to the accusations any longer and tried to escape the mob, but my eyes became transfixed on the torchbearer as he drew nearer the pile of faggots that surrounded the stake. I found myself yelling at him to stay away. When I saw the poor woman being tied to the stake I began screaming for mercy for her, but my pleas were drowned out by the cheers that were bellowed out by the crowd. The faggots were struck and the flames leaped from one wood bundle to the next. My pleas turned to prayers as I prayed for her soul and for these sinning people. Overcome by grief and panic, I found myself fighting to get to the front of the crowd so that she might hear my words. As I neared the pyre, I saw that she had managed to free her hands, but for all her efforts it was too late. The flames were engulfing her body as her screams became louder and louder. Her eyes were tightly closed, and she began to arch her back. I saw her hands rushing to her throat as she thrashed her head from side to side, and I could see her lips mouthing some words. She could have been saying, "Oh, Lord, curse these people for what they are doing to me." Then she was overcome with the smoke and fainted.

I fell to my knees and prayed.

"Durand, is that you down there? Get up, man, before you get crushed to death."

"Jacques, help me up. I don't seem to have the strength to move. Take me away from here."

"Isabelle told me that you had come to look for me. I'm sorry you had to get tied up with all this. I know how you feel about this sort of thing. Come on; let's get you home."

Once back at Jacques's house, I asked to be excused and went directly to the loft, where I lay on the bed that they had given me. I began to pray, hoping that the prayers would help to calm myself, but instead I found myself choking with sobs. I pulled the pillow over my head to stifle my cries and thrust my face hard against the mattress to drown the tears, but that brought no relief. I ached with sobs. I beat my clenched fists against the bed, but that didn't help either. I don't know how long I lay there in this state before I felt arms around me and Isabelle Romée pulling me close. She was rocking me back and forth, pressing my head against her shoulder.

"There, Durand, there," she whispered, and her voice was choked with sorrow, too. "I knew you shouldn't have gone looking for Jacques. I thought this might happen." For a long time we stayed so, she whispering soothing words such as one might use to a baby, rocking me slightly, wiping my face and her own with a corner of her apron. The storm of weeping slowed until there were but a few last shuddering sobs.

"I didn't realize that seeing a burning up close would affect me so."

"Oh yes, Durand. This is why I never go anywhere near one. I never want to know what it is like. Just seeing you in this manner makes me realize how terrifying it is. Jacques is preparing a bite for us to eat, and the boys have gone off to the village well to collect water. Come, Durand. Come join us; we can talk about more cheerful matters."

The d'Arcs' house was very comfortable, made from stone and rubble, with a loft above the main room in which the children slept. Jacques and Isabelle could live in such a fine house due to the position Jacques held in the community. Not only was he the collector of taxes for the town's overlord, but he also held the position as head watchman for the safety of the village folk and their livestock—no easy feat during these times when raids were becoming almost a monthly occurrence.

Isabelle placed baby Joan into my arms while she went to relieve her husband at the fireplace. "Go talk to Durand," she said as she took the bread from him. Although the meal that was prepared by the d'Arcs looked inviting, I had little appetite to eat it.

"So, Durand, what's the talk in Vaucouleurs? Do you think we're going to make it against the English? These raids are beginning to take their toll on our people. The peasant farmers around here do not have much more to lose. What little extra they save the English knights plunder. What little food they have now is not enough to last until the next harvest. I'm afraid we can't stand up to many more attacks."

"It's the same everywhere, Jacques. People talk of the great misery spreading through France as the English move from one region to the next plundering our lands. There are even rumors circulating that our beloved Catholic church, which has long been a source of inspiration to our people, is being corrupted by wealth and power."

"Heaven forbid, I hope this is not so."

"I think it is. Some of my friends who have lost confidence in the state are now turning their backs on the Church as well. I feel sorry for them."

"Isabelle's biggest fear is that the plague will return. If the Black Death strikes again, France will suffer greatly. People have very little food, they're weak and starving, and that means their resistance is low to such a terrible disease."

Isabelle was right. Throughout our history Black Death has struck again and again, causing widespread death and destruction. Victims of Black Death find that their bodies begin swelling all over. Soon afterward they die. It's an awful sight. Practically overnight their flesh turns black, and they die within days. No town or village has been able to escape the plague once it arrives. And when it hits, one begins to hear horrible stories—tales of corpses being piled high in the streets because they couldn't be buried or burned quick enough, stories of wild animals coming into town to feast on the rotting bodies.

During the last plague many thought that the world was coming to an end because of the huge number of people that were falling victim to the disease. Others went around torching the houses of those families who had members die from the ailment, thinking that they were preventing the plague from spreading any further. And there were others who felt that God was punishing the French for their sins and had abandoned them. These people turned to the Church for help, but it soon became apparent that even the Church and its surroundings weren't safe havens from the plague. The most bitter and disillusioned members of society turned to the devil for help, defying the Church that had failed them. Strange witchcraft rituals sprang up all over France, causing the men of the Church to become alarmed. Such men became fanatical in searching out such rituals and the people behind them. Many innocent people were investigated for such insignificant things as using herbs for cooking or a simple spell to cure a sick goat. Many people were burned at the stake for unwarranted charges or to satisfy the egos of those in power. It was a terrible time for all.

"Do you know what France needs?" said Isabelle, addressing the two men sitting at the table. "We need a good leader that can organize and train our armies to drive out our enemy. We have been at war with the English for almost a hundred years, and still we cannot defeat them. They seem to know our every move before we make it. There has to be someone out there who can fill this post."

"Easier said than done, Isabelle," replied her husband.

"War has been on the lips of our children for a long time now. Battles and skirmishes have been a way of life for the French for so long it's hard to imagine it any other way," said Isabelle. "Clashes with the English and Burgundian soldiers have left our lovely countryside devastated. There has to be a way out of this."

Isabelle may have had a point. The kingdom of France has no strong leader to lead us to victory against our foe. Charles VI and his armies have had little success in stopping the English from marching back and forth across our coun-

tryside burning crops, looting villages, and committing murders as they go.

I woke after a short night's sleep to the sound of someone chanting morning prayers out in the street. They sounded wonderful and momentarily made me forget about the events of the previous day, but I was still tired and tried to slip back into sleep. I felt exhausted, as if I had not slept at all. I pulled the covers up, but the prayer caller's voice could not be blocked out, so I arose, washed my hands and face in the wooden bucket that Isabelle had provided for my use, and got dressed. To my surprise, I was the last one up. Out of the window I could see the whole family busy about their morning chores. Even baby Joan strapped to her mother's back was wide awake, obviously having already had her morning meal. As I looked at them, my stomach rumbled in protest and I realized that I was ravenous. I went into the kitchen, slipped a little bread from the scullery, and devoured it.

After breakfast I popped out into the street to see if the village had recovered from the previous evening's events; the air was thick with mist. The banners that had been proudly displayed the night before now hung limp and pale, as if the fog had robbed them of their color. The wet cobbles were slippery; however, the few people who were about went on their way paying little regard to the wet conditions. It wasn't until midmorning that the mist burned off, leaving the warmth of the sun to heat up the village. Domrémy was back to normal.

Shortly after lunch, as we were seated out in the yard making polite conversation and while Jacques's boys were preparing my horse for my return journey to Burey, we heard shouting noises coming from the street.

"Jacques, I think someone is calling your name," I told him.

"Monsieur d'Arc! Monsieur d'Arc! Can you hear me? The English are coming! Regnault was out riding and saw them approaching the backwoods from the west on the far side of the river. He thinks they're heading our way. Shall I ring out a warning on the church bells?"

"Yes! And do it quickly!" Jacques shouted.

"We'll collect the stock!" the boys shouted as they were running out the gate.

"Start driving them out of town on the eastbound road, and leave two behind this time!" Jacques called after them.

By the look of the boys' swift actions this procedure had been conducted many times before. They knew exactly what was required of them. "It's another raiding party," said Jacques. "I wonder why they are back so soon; we're not ready for them. Quickly, Durand, collect your things, mount your horse, and head out of town. Hurry! Go back to Burey. This is not your fight. You need not be here. We have a good twenty minutes before they reach the village."

"No, Jacques. Give me a weapon. I can fight as well," I replied.

"No, Durand, this time we won't confront them. Sometimes we just have to flee and save what we can. They're not here for blood. I'm sure they're just back for food. We'll leave a couple of cows in the field for them to kill and take. When they move on we'll return to our homes. I just hope they don't torch any of our buildings like they did the last time they were here."

"Durand, watch the baby for a moment while I throw a few things into the wagon," said Isabelle.

Before I had time to think, Joan was thrust into my arms and her mother was running toward the back of the house, where Jacques was busy hitching the horse to the cart. I could hear similar shouts coming from the neighboring houses and knew that similar scenes had to be going on in their backyards as well. The whole village was preparing to leave. As I stood there with Joan in my arms, pondering over how these people could live this way, my thoughts were constantly being interrupted by Isabelle as she dashed from the house and rushed toward the wagon with a pile of clothes or food. She seemed to know exactly what to take and what to leave behind.

"Do you need any help?"

"No thanks, Durand. I'm almost done."

I was amazed at how calmly they were treating the whole affair. Although they were hurrying, there certainly wasn't that sense of panic that I would expect there to be. "Well, little one," I motioned to the baby, "you've only been in this world for a few days and already you're learning how to beat the enemy. Welcome to reality, Joan. Let's hope you learn how to cope with it as calmly as the rest of your family."

I couldn't bring myself to leave for Burey, abandoning the family under such circumstances, so I stayed and helped the boys drive the livestock away from the village and into the eastern woodlands for safety. Jacques was right. The Burgundians were only after food, and the cattle left in the fields were enough to satisfy their needs this time. After a few hours they moved off with their stolen meat and the villagers returned to their homes unharmed.

And so was life in Domrémy, with the villagers living

from one raid to the next. Not all raids went as this one did, however. Often the folk of Domrémy put up a fight, which would result in a bloody battle, loss of life occurring on both sides. It has been this way for almost a hundred years. When was it all going to end and where was this young maiden that our prophecies said was going to arrive and save us? She had better come soon or there won't be a France worth saving. It will all belong to the English.

Chapter Two
A Simple Village Girl

There is between Coussey and Vaucouleurs a young girl who before another year will cause the crowning of the king of France.

Jacques d'Arc reporting:

Joan woke and lay in the snug warmth of her coat, curled under the bending branches of an oak tree. Her distaff, which she used for spinning wool, lay at her side. The wind had stopped blowing. Silence lay thick as a pile rug on the hearth. It was her turn to tend to her father's cattle, and she was out in the cold. However, she didn't mind, as she loved being outdoors. Before she had fallen asleep, the wind had threatened to topple every tree in sight, but now there wasn't a trace of it. No dried leaves stirred or old branches brushed together. Even the sound of the nearby river seemed to be muffled by the silence. A covey of little brown birds hopped nearby as she lay watching them for a while.

Joan yawned and crawled out from her cozy nook to check on the cattle. They were grazing happily nearby and had not wandered off at all. As she stood, she stretched, then bent to pick up her distaff and ball of wool. The brown birds flew twittering from the ground up into the branches of the large oak tree that had been her temporary mantle. "OK, you lot, there's no need to fuss. It's time for me to move on anyway. It's all yours." She motioned to the birds. As she spoke, she looked toward the village and saw the outlines of two boys heading her way. She could tell by the way they walked and how they fooled about that they were two of her three brothers, Jean and Pierre.

"Hi, Joan!" one of them called from a distance. "It's time for us to take over. Papa wants you back at the house; he has a chore for you."

Joan loved helping me out, so she skipped merrily back to the house to see what I had in mind. She saw that the wagon had been hitched, which was usually an indication that we were going out collecting. She often went out with me on tax collecting trips for the landlord, but she would always stay in the wagon when I stopped at a house. Many times people would refuse to open the door when they saw me coming or would shout out nasty remarks as I approached. Joan preferred not to hear their angry words.

I saw my daughter skipping across the fields and stopped loading the wagon to watch her. I couldn't get over how sweet a girl my daughter had grown into. How loving and kind she was to everyone she met. I very rarely heard her speak harshly of anyone, which was why, I knew, she was loved by all. At ten years old she was very helpful to both me and my wife, laboring just as hard as any of our sons. I marveled at how she managed to stay so cheerful in spite of the troubles our country was in. The constant skirmishes our village experienced did not seem to dampen her spirits one bit.

"Papa, are we going out collecting?" she called from across the road.

"Yes, we are."

"Could you give me a few minutes? I want to stop by the church and offer up a few prayers at the shrine."

"All right, but don't be long. We have many people to visit." This was something else about my daughter at which

I marveled. She had this great love and respect for the Lord. It was just as well the village church was just across the road from our house, as she spent much of her time there in prayer. She loved to hear its bells ringing out their call for prayer, and when they sounded they attracted her as insects are attracted to firelight. If she was nearby when they rang, she dropped everything and went to the church. If she was out in the field attending the cows, she would make it a point to stop in later. I admire her so much for this devotion. "What took you so long?"

"Oh, Papa, you know I wasn't long; and besides, whenever we go collecting, I always like to pray for protection. You never know what might happen while we are out."

I let my daughter chatter on as we headed out of town together, but I wasn't really listening to her. I had more pressing matters to think over in my mind. Since the battle with the English at Agincourt, where we French suffered a humiliating defeat by losing thousands of noble knights, things had continued to deteriorate for my country. Even the new treaty that the Duke of Burgundy and Queen Isabelle had signed with the English was turning out to be one huge treacherous plot by them against France. They were calling this pact the Treaty of Troyes, which in the beginning we had great hopes for, but now we know it as a conspiracy against the country. "You know, Joan, our king may have his problems, but he is still our king; we need to look out for him."

"You haven't heard a word I've been saying to you, have you, Papa?"

"No, Joan, I haven't. I've been thinking about the English. I think that they are here to stay and there is nothing we can do about it. They now control most of the rich, fertile lands of the north, including Paris, and are growing stronger by the day."

"Papa, it's out of our hands. There is nothing we can do

here in Domrémy. We will have to leave it in the hands of the Lord."

"Maybe you're right." This was Joan's answer to everything she couldn't understand. "Maybe He, too, can see the misery this Treaty of Troyes has caused us."

Because of this treacherous treaty with the English, Queen Isabelle had disinherited her very own son, Prince Charles, from the throne of France in favor of the English king. The prince's life was in great danger. We heard that some of his loyal followers had to smuggle him out of Paris and he was now living in exile near the Loire River. The scene in France was indeed grave.

Joan, like most of the young women in Domrémy, followed a set daily routine, which included both house chores and farm work, toiling from dawn to dusk to harvest enough food for the family to eat. However, not every waking moment was devoted to work. On occasions the village overlords, the Bourlemonts, would hold festivals that were full of fun and excitement for their land laborers. On such days the overlords would hire performers to entertain; jesters and jugglers would roam through the crowd and perform tricks. Animal trainers would sometimes appear with monkeys and bears to entertain as well. These were times for Joan and the rest of us to forget the worries of the day and do nothing but eat, drink, and socialize. We loved these days. The forest that surrounded the Bourlemonts' castle was a popular site for the celebrations, as under the trees was a favorite picnic spot for all. We men would gather around each other to discuss the latest political events while the older women prepared the food that would be eaten later. The young would sing, tell stories, and dance around the trees.

"Mama, look; the musicians are playing their flutes, and the women have started dancing already. Come; let's go join in."

"Oh, Joan, I'm too old to join in with those games now. You go ahead and have fun. I need to visit the sacred fountain and see if I can't be cured of some of these aches and pains."

"OK, see you later." She could see her good friends Rachelle and Michelle enjoying the fun of the dance so was eager to join them.

"Joan, come dance around the Fairies' Trees with us!" shouted Michelle when she saw Joan approaching.

"I'm coming," Joan replied, as she ran to join hands with the others as they danced around the huge beech tree reenacting an ancient pagan ritual. As she danced, she could see other young men and women of the village sitting nearby making flower garlands to hang from the same trees. Joan knew that what they were doing was a ritual that had been performed by young people in their village for generations. Many of the villagers felt that the Fairies' Trees held special powers for them and the dances that they performed were pleasing to the spirits beyond. In return these spirits would help the village in some way or other. Joan was only too happy to join in, as she loved tradition.

"Look, everybody! A wandering vendor has turned up. Let's go and see what he has in his wagon to sell!" yelled one of the dancers as he broke from the circle and headed toward the vendor's wagon.

When I saw the vendor, I knew my daughter would be happy, as a traveling vendor usually meant baskets full of little trinkets and images of saints for sale. As I saw her racing toward me, I knew exactly what she would be asking of me.

"Hello, you lot," responded the peddler to their eager questions. "Are you having fun today? I didn't mean to distract you from your dancing." The children crowded around and helped him unload his table and baskets off his wagon. "I hope you all have lots of coins to trade with me today. I have brought special things from Paris. Items that I have sold nowhere else in France. I have been saving them especially for you folk."

Joan smiled to herself as she listened to him speak. These vendors always said things like this to try to sell their wares. "Do you have any images of the two virgin saints, Saint Catherine and Saint Margaret?"

"Joan, you always ask for the same things," interrupted Michelle. "He has lots of other things as well, you know. Why not buy a lovely comb or a colorful scarf for yourself instead? Haven't you enough statues of those two saints already?"

"Yes, I know, but I do love them so much."

I knew that it wouldn't be long before my daughter would be over to ask for a coin or two to buy another set of miniature statues. She was especially devoted to the two virgin saints, Catherine and Margaret, and if that vendor had either, Joan wouldn't leave without them in her possession. It was the statue of Saint Margaret in our village church that was Joan's favorite. "So what pretty thing have you found for yourself this time, Joan?"

"Oh, Papa, you know I don't like to buy all that fancy stuff. No, I would like to buy a statue."

"Let me guess. Is it Saint Catherine or is it Saint Margaret this time?" I loved to tease my daughter, and the men around me joined in with laughter as well. They all knew of Joan's devotion and loved her for it.

For us adults in the village there was always great excitement whenever one of the wandering vendors turned up. Peddlers usually carried a wealth of information as they traveled. They brought valuable news from the west as to what was happening with the war.

So after the young ones had finished inspecting this vendor's trinkets and the women had examined every item of clothing he carried, we men surrounded him. We hung on his every word, the vendor enjoying his position of importance.

"Have you been in Paris lately?" asked one of the villagers.

"Yes, of course. Paris is where I buy most of my merchandise from. I'm there regularly."

"And what has happened to our beloved Prince Charles? They say that Queen Isabelle has disinherited her very own son from the throne of France in favor of the English king. Is this true?"

"Oh yes, indeed it is. He's no longer living in the city because he fears for his life."

"We heard that some of his loyal followers had to smuggle him out of Paris and he is now living in exile near the Loire River."

"Once again, this is correct. He feels that he is safer there than in his beloved city."

"Then his mother has done him a great injustice."

"Most of France would agree with you, sir."

The talk with the vendor would usually go on for hours, with the entire village surrounding him as a captivated audience, listening to his every word. Such men were sometimes the only means of news in the village for weeks on end.

They were valuable not only because they brought news from the capital, but also because of the news they brought from neighboring districts. Knowing what one's neighbors thought sometimes determined the outcome of a decision the villagers had to make on a particular issue. Only after the vendor had been exhausted of all his news would the festival continue. Usually the vendors themselves were entertainers, and often they would pull out an instrument and strike up a tune or two. The children would dance around them and clap their hands while we adults would retire to the nearest tree to sit and discuss the news that we had just heard.

It was one such vendor that brought the news to Domrémy that both the mad King Charles of France and King Henry of England had died * and that the entire country was in a turmoil over the deaths. At first nobody believed the vendor, but soon a royal messenger passed through the village, making the news official. After hearing the announcement that the messenger had proclaimed in the market square, I headed home to inform my family that the news was true. "Isabelle, this has to be France's darkest hour. With our king dead, his son Prince Charles living in exile, and Queen Isabelle favoring the English, things do not look good for our royal family and France," I told my wife.

"There must be something the people can do," replied Isabelle. "I heard a rumor today that King Henry's infant son is being hailed as the new king of England and France. Surely this can't be so?"

"I'm afraid that it's no longer a rumor. That's the rest of the message I came to tell you about. The English are proclaiming this child to be the king of France as well."

*It was in 1422 that both these kings died.

"A baby can't be king," Pierre remarked.

"The messenger said that his uncle, the Duke of Bedford, is to rule as regent until the child-king is of age to rule for himself."

"What about our own Prince Charles? He is the rightful heir to our throne. Not some child-king way off in England," said Joan.

"I think you're right, Joan," I said, "and I'm sure most of France thinks the way you do. Charles has been well educated and well trained for the job."

"People say that he would make a terrible king, though," said Isabelle. "That he lacks confidence and courage and that he couldn't make a decision if his life depended upon it."

"This may be so, but he should still be our king. He's French," remarked Joan.

"They also say that he employs a whole household of fancy courtiers and astrologers from whom he seeks advice when he needs to make up his mind on anything. Not the sort of leader we need in France right now. But you're right, Joan," said Isabelle. "We need a French king here in France. We don't need an English goddon * to rule over us."

The English themselves probably felt that the war they had been fighting intermittently with we French for the past one hundred years was finally coming to an end. They believed that they were in France to stay whether we wanted them there or not. Their general opinion probably was that should we French try to make a stronghold attempt to win back our lands, we lacked an officer knowledgeable enough to lead us. What the English did not bargain on, however, was that they had an ancient prophecy against them. The

*English soldiers were often referred to as "goddons" because of their constant use of the slang *goddamn*.

prophecy stated that a young female liberator was at hand, a liberator to come from a most unlikely source. They were soon to feel the effects of this prediction.

Chapter Three
Voices from Heaven

You have been chosen by God to go to the rescue of Dauphin Charles and the kingdom of France.

Pierre d'Arc reporting:

It was still a little dark when I opened my eyes, sat up, and looked around the loft. The bed next to mine belonged to my brother Jean, and it had already been vacated. Our plan was to be up and ready to leave well before the sun had begun to rise, but I had slept in. I vaguely recalled Jean shaking my shoulder sometime earlier, but I must have fallen asleep again. My eyelids burned from tiredness and my cheeks felt stiff, but I prepared to get up. I cocked my head and listened to see if anyone else was stirring but the house was quiet, which meant that Jean must have been outside already preparing weapons. I was a little afraid to stand in case my movements shattered the stillness of the morning, so I sat on my bed for a few moments longer and thought about what the morning would hold.

Carefully I eased myself off the bed and dressed in my tunic and leggings before descending the loft stairs to the main hall. The rest of the family lay sound asleep as I passed through the exit door. Outside I saw my brother Jean loading our backpacks with stones.

"You sleep well?" he asked.

"I guess I did." I could see that Jean had that look of concern on his face.

"You don't look too good," he said. "Are you certain you're up for this?"

"Sure."

"Papa would be mad if he found out that we were going to Maxey on a raid."

"He'll never find out," I replied softly as I tucked my tunic under my belt and laced up my boots. "Thanks for this," he remarked, as I picked up my heavy backpack and placed it over my shoulders.

I felt a touch of guilt as we walked out of the yard to our planned rendezvous with the others. I hated doing something that went against my father's wishes; however, I hated the Burgundians even more.

Long before we reached the outer limits of the village we could see that the rest of the gang had already begun to gather. "Well, it's about time!" one of the gang members yelled as they saw us d'Arc boys approaching. "We've been waiting for you two. You're the last ones."

The youths of Domrémy often clashed in local fights with the youths of the Burgundian village of Maxey, which was just across the river. My friends and I would sneak across, usually just before dawn, to attack the Maxey boys as they headed out to the pasturelands with their herds. We would carry sticks and stones to use as weapons. Sometimes our battles would be bloody, with members from both sides receiving cuts and bruises from the attack. Jacques and Isabelle did not approve of this sort of carrying-on.

The sun had been up for roughly an hour before the gang reached the outskirts of Maxey. We knew that our enemy would be along at any moment herding cattle and sheep. Our gang split up into pairs, the way we had done many times before, and made our way silently through the now-familiar territory. Our plans were to cover each of the main tracks leaving the village. The Maxey boys themselves had taken to walking in pairs since the attacks on them had become more frequent.

"Jean, I hear the cattle coming," I said.

"Can you see how many herders there are, Pierre?"

"No." I could hear their muffled voices but could not make out what they were saying. Before I could think out a plan, Jean was motioning me forward.

"Pierre, you ready? Let's go get them," he whispered over his shoulder.

I sucked in my breath and started forward, one fist clenched around my wooden staff and the other around a stone. We ran forward with gusto, eager to be the first to claim a victim. I could now see the cattle herders clearly, and they could see me. There were three of them. For a moment I hesitated, knowing that Jean and I were outnumbered, but seeing my brother racing on with such gusto gave me the courage I needed to continue.

"It's the Domrémy gang," I heard one of the Burgundians yell as they turned to brace themselves for the surprise attack.

"What are you doing here?" another shouted as they bunched together. "This is not your turf."

"Just letting you know we plan to travel wherever we please. No one's going to tell us where we can and cannot go," Jean answered in measured tones.

"This is our territory. You got no call coming here."

"Says who, you dogs!" Jean spat his words out as if they were poison, and the fight was on.

"Well, take this then!" one of them shouted, but before he could raise his wooden rod, Jean had him pummeled and dropped by a quick uppercut under the jaw. He lay on the ground wincing in pain. With one down that left us evenly matched.

I followed Jean's example by slamming my opponent across the shoulders with my staff before he could land a decent punch on me. But unfortunately, that was not enough to take him down and he came at me with the full force of his body. Both the staff and the stone were knocked from my hands, so I knew I had to rely on my fists. Grunts and smacking noises filled the air, and by the number of impacts that were making contact with my face, I knew that I was coming out second best. For a split moment I felt nothing, but when I came to I was lying on the ground looking up at Jean about to take an almighty swing at my opponent. Moments later this boy was on the ground beside me.

"If I knew you were going to take time out to sleep I would have left you at home." Jean grinned as he helped me up off the ground. I could feel the warm blood spilling from my nose. The three Maxey boys had picked themselves up off the ground and run off in the direction of their village, muttering curses as they left. With very little warning at all, from out of the trees came a fourth boy, a little larger than the others. He came racing at us at top speed.

"Watch out, Jean!" I yelled, as I saw the boy charging. His arms were raised, and he was ready to strike. Jean lowered his chin to take the onslaught, but the thrust of the charge was too great and it sent Jean sprawling. He had leaped onto my brother's back and began choking him with both hands. Jean did a quick series of jerks with his upper body, and the boy went tumbling. He hit the ground hard but was soon on his feet again. Jean himself jumped up, raised his fists, and went in for the battle. For a moment Jean and the Maxey boy circled each other like wrestlers looking for a good hold, and then Jean took a flying leap forward. He landed on the other boy, knocking him flat on his back, but the boy recovered quickly, and they rolled back and forth on the ground, pounding each other.

I watched in amazement as my brother tried to outmaneuver his rival. It was a remarkable fight. I wanted to help but found myself unable to move. The fight went on for what seemed ages, as the boys were evenly matched, until Jean finally got the upper hand. At one stage Jean was on top of his opponent when I saw the boy try to reach into his pocket with one hand for what looked like a knife. But he never had a chance. With one sharp blow, Jean had landed his mark. There was a loud gasp, and the boy slumped to the ground.

"Are you all right?" I shouted as I scrambled to my brother's side and began wiping the blood off his face. "That was some fight. For a moment I thought you were done for."

"I would have been if he had gotten that into me." Jean directed my attention to the ground. I looked down and saw the boy's knife lying on the ground. "We need to be a bit more careful next time. We had better find the others and make haste before more unexpected fighters arrive from the village. I think we pounded them good this time."

Joan saw us, her two brothers, entering the backyard and from our appearance knew exactly what we had been up to. "You two had better pray for thanks that Papa is away at the landlord's. If he finds out what you've been doing you will be in trouble. Just look at the sight of your clothes. I suppose you expect Mama or me to mend them. You had better wash those cuts and have Mama look at them, and you had better hope that she doesn't tell Papa." Joan loved us dearly and hated to see us hurt or in trouble with our father.

She was seeing less and less of us lately now that she had taken to helping our mother with the household chores and was spending less time with the cattle. Our father said that we boys were old enough to handle the herd by ourselves and Joan needed to spend more time with her mother and learn more of the household duties. However, Joan didn't really mind, because as they worked inside, our mother was giving her religious instruction at the same time. She learned about not only events that happened in the Bible, but also important prayers of the Catholic faith. She was so keen to learn that our mother had only needed to recite the Lord's Prayer a few times before Joan had memorized it by heart. She went on to learn the Hail Mary and the Catholic creed, in a similar fashion. Our mother was exceedingly pleased. "Go out and spend time with the boys, Joan," Mother said, "while I prepare the nightly meal."

"You're becoming quite the lady around the house, aren't you, Joan? We had better start looking for a husband for you," I teased, as we saw her heading toward us wearing an apron.

"Very funny, I must say," snapped Joan. "Do you want to know something? I don't care if I never get married. I'm quite happy as I am."

"You're thirteen years old," added Jean quickly. "There are plenty of dashing young men out there who would be only too happy to tie the knot with you." We boys giggled as we saw our sister growing angry at Jean's audacious remarks.

"Will you boys stop it. I don't need you to be matchmaking for me, thank you."

"With the amount of time you spend in the garden reciting prayers, dear sister, it's a wonder you have any time at all to get to know any young men." We boys laughed as she scurried off toward the garden to evade our smart comments.

My sister did spend a lot of time in our father's garden, and it was here, in her thirteenth year, that Joan was to receive the first word of the momentous task that lay ahead of her. These words came in the form of a mystical experience that was to change her life forever. It was a lovely summer day, just after the church bells had sounded the beginning of noontime.

"Joan, are you coming in for lunch?" I shouted as my brother and I headed toward the house. I could see that she was on her knees in prayerlike fashion, except this time her head was not bowed as normal but was gazing upward instead. I thought about this for a brief moment, then brushed it from my mind and went inside without her. Had we boys have known what our sister was experiencing right then, we might have rushed up to her to investigate.

"Why didn't your sister come in with you?" our mother asked as she placed the bread on the table.

"We asked her to come, but it's as if our words passed right over her head."

Indeed, at that time Joan's attention was not that of the living. She was captivated by a brilliant light that had appeared before her. She was being spoken to by a magnificent celestial being: Michael the Archangel. He was telling her that she had to be good and that she had to go to church often. He spoke to her of the pitiful condition that the kingdom of France was in and how God needed her help to resolve it. Michael also told her that in the not too distant future she would ride to the aid of Prince Charles, the Dauphin, and with a band of soldiers she would bring him to be crowned the true king of France, at Rheims.

Joan was extremely frightened and wasn't sure that she should stay and listen to the archangel, but every muscle in her body was captivated by his aura and she couldn't leave him even if she wanted to. "Please, I am only a peasant girl without the skills needed to perform the tasks you mention. I have no knowledge of how to ride a horse or to command a band of soldiers. You must be speaking to the wrong person."

The vision slowly disappeared after telling her that she was not to worry and that God would help her. Joan could not believe what she had just experienced and was completely overcome; she fell to the ground weeping like an infant.

"Go get your sister, Pierre. Tell her that her lunch is getting cold," Isabelle muttered as she began clearing the table.

"OK." I passed out of the house and into the garden to look for Joan. She was still where we had last seen her, but this time I could tell that she was terribly distressed about something. By the way that she lay on the ground sobbing I thought that she might have been bitten by a snake or some other wild creature. I ran as fast as I could to her side to give assistance. "What's the matter, Joan? Let me help you up. Where are you hurt?"

"Nowhere, Pierre. It is my heart that is burdened."

"Is that all. I thought that you had been seriously maimed in some way. Would you like me to help you inside? Come; let me help you up. I'm not a very good listener, but you can tell Mama all about it."

"No. I prefer to sit here for a little longer. I have nothing to tell anybody."

"Your lunch is getting cold."

"I have no need of lunch today."

Joan was filled with both fear and happiness over her recent supernatural experience but too afraid to tell anyone about it. She refused to tell our parents, her brothers, or even the village priest with whom she had confession regularly. She felt that the vision and the words that she had heard were for her alone. As time passed, her supernatural visitor came more and more frequently, and she began to look forward to his voice. Several times a week Michael appeared before her, always surrounded by the brilliant light. Each time he came he would tell her of her mission. During one of his appearances he told her that she would soon be visited by her two favorite saints. Saint Catherine and Saint Margaret would come to advise her on the task that lay before her. He always told Joan that they would be the bearers of messages straight from God.

"Joan, aren't you spending far too much time outdoors lately? I hardly see you these days," said our mother one night over dinner. "I have many chores around this place, but you never seem to be around to help. Where do you go? Are you meeting someone?"

"I spend a lot of my time at the church, Mama."

"What do you do there?"

"I pray, Mama."

"You do? Well, I suppose that's OK then."

"Or sometimes I walk over to the forest that surrounds the Bourlemonts' castle to sit alone and meditate." Joan contemplated telling her devout mother about her heavenly conversations, but she decided against it. She was glad that no one suspected what was happening inside her. People might not understand and might ridicule her or, worse still, not believe her. However, in her heart she never doubted once that her Voices came from God.

As Michael promised, the Voices of her two favorite saints began to arrive. At first Joan only heard their voices, but later the Voices were accompanied by visions, appearing before her as Michael did. She loved it when they came and hated it when they left. Often she begged for them to take her with them.

"Joan, are you coming with us? There's a picnic for the

youth of the village in the forest near the castle. Come on; your friends will think that you have deserted them if you don't come. Why, just yesterday Michelle asked me if you were sick; she says she hasn't seen you for a while. Come with us." Jean was trying to coax Joan into joining the group.

Joan didn't really feel like going, as she had found it hard to be around her friends lately, but she decided to go anyway. "All right, wait for me and I'll slip on a clean skirt and pack a bag of lunch for us to take."

"No, don't bother; the Bourlemonts are supplying picnic food for all. They say that we just have to turn up at the forest and that food and wine will be plentiful."

"Well, that's very nice of them. OK, I'll be down in a minute."

"Joan is that you? We thought that you had left town. Come and dance with us around the Fairies' Trees!" hollered Rachelle as she saw the d'Arcs arriving at the picnic grounds.

"Hi there!" Joan yelled back, but she was in no mood to go dancing. She joined in for a couple of rounds before slipping away to a quieter setting.

Joan spent less and less time with her friends as her inner self began to demand more of her attention. She began to annoy her family and friends as she kept making excuses why she could not attend a certain festivity or a ceremony. She no longer did what normal sixteen-year-old girls in the village did. Instead she would slip off to a secluded little chapel not far from her village, where she could be alone to commune with her voices and not be fearful of being seen. Her voices became more and more frequent and more and more insistent that her hour of preparation was at hand, that it was time for her to go and seek out the exiled Dauphin Charles, the uncrowned king of France, and offer her assistance. She pleaded with them once again (as she had done when Michael first appeared before her), saying that she did not have the skills for the job that they were asking of her. Their answers were the same as before. God would help her. Her saints ordained that she first go to Vaucouleurs and get help from Sire de Baudricourt, the governor. Once she was there, everything would be made clear to her. Joan was still not convinced that she could do this; however, her Voices insisted that she could do this. She need only to start.

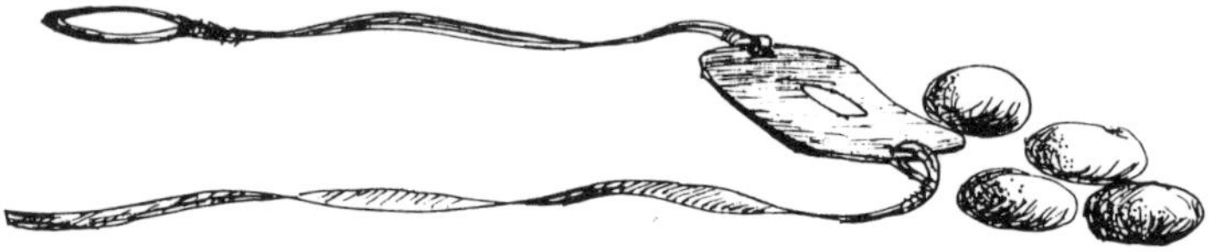

Chapter Four
It Is for This That I Was Born

Her mission came from God—given a year and a little more of usefulness.

Durand Laxart reporting:

I was extremely upset when news reached me in Burey that the village of Domrémy had suffered the worst attack yet by the Burgundian soldiers. I feared for the safety of my cousins that lived there and tried hard to learn of their whereabouts. I went out onto the road and questioned everyone I could that had come from that direction. I learned from travelers returning from Greux, a neighboring village, that the Burgundians' attack had occurred a week previously and since then the soldiers had completely taken over the village. From a distance one traveler reported that he could tell that the villagers had all fled, as the only people in sight were those in uniforms. The cattle that had been grazing in the surrounding fields had all disappeared as well. Another traveler reported seeing billows of smoke in the skies over the village and said that he knew for a fact that the inhabitants of Domrémy had all fled south, but did not know of their condition. I would only learn later what had taken place.

"Monsieur d'Arc, may I speak with you please? It is very important," a man asked my cousin.

"Yes, of course, Louis. Please come on in."

"As you currently hold the position of head watchman for the safety of our village folk and our livestock, I feel I must tell you this grave piece of news that has just come to my attention."

"Please go on, Louis; you look very distressed. Are you all right? Come in and sit down."

"As you know, I have cousins that live over the river in Maxey, in enemy territory. A traveler has just stopped by my house with a message from them that is very serious indeed and may need immediate action. Their message states that we need to prepare ourselves at once for an imminent attack. The Burgundian soldiers are this moment preparing their weapons for an all-out assault on us tomorrow. They plan to take all our livestock this time. They are in desperate need of food to feed their huge armies up north."

"This is indeed serious news, Louis. Did they say anything else?"

"Yes. The soldiers not only plan to take our livestock, but also much of our household possessions. The messenger urges that we not waste a moment of time, but pack up all that we can carry and leave tonight for safer regions."

"Then let's not wait a moment longer. Thanks, Louis, for the warning. You did right by coming to me at once. We need to inform the town of this news immediately. Could you rush to the church and ring the bells? I'll go straight to the town square and wait for everyone to come."

Jacques had organized a set of bell patterns that were used as warning signals for the villagers. Everyone in Domrémy knew exactly what was expected of them for each pattern. What was being rung now indicated that all villagers needed to stop what they were doing and report to the town square for an important meeting. Jacques greeted them as they came.

"What's wrong, Jacques?" they asked as they joined the rest of the crowd milling around the square.

But Jacques urged them to wait until everyone was present before he made an announcement. As soon as he saw Louis, accompanied by the priest, arriving from the church, he began to tell them of their predicament. Louis's cousins across the border had often sent warnings to him of imminent danger and each time their warnings were justified, so the Domrémy citizens had no reason to take this one lightly either. "We have reason to believe that we will be attacked by the Burgundian soldiers early tomorrow morning. We also have reason to believe that this attack will be on a far larger scale than we have seen for a long time. The large English armies up north are in desperate need of food and equipment, and they plan to obtain some of these from us tomorrow morning."

"Then we need to be packed and be gone by tomorrow morning!" shouted someone from the crowd.

"I agree with you, sir. Which is why I want all stock in the field to be brought in, roped, and ready to leave at a moment's notice. All personal effects that you don't want to fall into the hands of the enemy need to be loaded onto wagons tonight, as before the sun comes up tomorrow we shall be on the road to Neufchâteau. I shall send word to them tonight of our present danger and to expect us. They have offered to help us in the past. Now we will take them up on their generous offer."

"How will we know if the Burgundian soldiers have come or not if we leave before we see them?" asked the same gentleman who had posed the first question. "They might not show up, and we would have packed up and left for nothing."

"Oh, I have a notion that they will be here. Two of my sons as well as myself will stay behind tomorrow after you have all left to wait and see if they turn up. We will depart long before they reach the river."

Louis's cousin's warning once again was true to form, and what Jacques and his boys observed from the nearby forest shortly after dawn horrified them. The Burgundians came by the dozens to plunder their village and came early hoping for a surprise attack. From a distance it looked like they were crazy men going from one house to the next setting them ablaze, probably in revenge for their lack of spoil. The d'Arc men watched in horror as they observed their neighborhood go up in smoke. Too stunned to talk, they turned their sights toward Neufchâteau and left, thankful that everyone else had left Domrémy long before dawn. This attack on their village was by far the worst attack they had ever known.

They were welcomed at the fortified town of Neufchâteau and each family was allocated a town's family to look after them. The d'Arcs were able to stay with the innkeeper, Madame la Rousse, so Joan and her mother soon found many ways to help the woman out.

After a week Jacques finally received word that the enemy had left Domrémy. He made the decision that it was time to take his people home and start rebuilding. When they arrived back, they were devastated. They found their village in ruins, with many of their homes burned to the ground; even the church had been destroyed by fire. Joan was very upset that the Burgundians could do such a thing to their beloved house of God. With no church to pray in, she began walking all the way to Greux, a village nearby, so that she could still worship in the house of the Lord.

Meanwhile, her Voices became very urgent. They kept urging her that she needed to begin her mission at once, that she needed to make plans to leave Domrémy. She began to realize that the moment of truth had finally arrived, that she must act now. In her mind she had looked on this task as something way off, something for the future, never quite to be met as a reality, but now it was time for her to do something about it. Her saints were telling her that she needed to seek out the Dauphin himself, that she needed to tell him that she had been sent by God, that he needed to hear for himself that God's plan for her was to have him crowned the king of France at Rheims.

"How can I do this?" she pleaded with the saints. "To find Dauphin Charles I would have to go all the way to Chinon, which is many days' ride into enemy territory. I don't know how to ride a horse. I have no idea how to find my way there, and if I do, they wouldn't let me in to see him; I'm only a poor peasant. Then, if I am granted an audience with him, he would only laugh at me and think me crazy. But more important, what am I going to tell my parents? They would think I have lost my mind and would whip me for speaking such craziness."

However, in spite of Joan's constant reservations her saints continued to be persistent, insisting that God would help her every move, that she would know what was expected of her when the time came. Her first mission was to go to Vaucouleurs and ask Robert de Baudricourt, the lord of Vaucouleurs, to provide her with an escort to go see the Dauphin. The lord would at first laugh at her but would eventually be persuaded. She must make haste, as she would only be given a little over a year to achieve everything God wished of her.

"Durand, you came. You got my message then."

"Yes, Joan. When I heard that the message was from you, I figured that you wanted to see me personally to inform me that soon we will hear wedding bells in our family. Am I right?"

"No, you are not. Please, I have little time to talk before Mama and Papa come in. Please, I need to go back to Burey with you. I will tell you the reason later. Ask my parents if I can return with you to help your wife, as they know she is in poor health. Please ask them. I will explain later."

"Joan, this sounds urgent. Are you all right?"

"Yes, Durand, I am. Please ask. They will permit me leave if you ask."

"OK."

"I have never disobeyed my parents before, Durand, and I hate to do it now, but I am on a mission for God, so it has to be all right."

I was too stunned by her statement to inquire then and there as to exactly what she meant. However, I saw how serious she was, so at the first opportunity I asked the d'Arcs if they could spare their daughter for a while. They agreed and we two left for Burey immediately, on Joan's insistence. As we walked, Joan told her incredible story. I was too startled to reply; I listened intently, without comment, until she had ended. "I believe you, Joan, but how will we ever explain this to anybody and have them believe us?"

"Cousin Durand, I need your help to get me started on

my mission. Burey is not that far from Vaucouleurs. Please take me there and arrange an audience for me with Sire Baudricourt. He is the one person who could secure my passage to Chinon. Please, Durand, help me. I'm sure God would grant you many graces for your help."

"With a submission like that, how could I refuse you, Joan?" I began to see a side of my cousin I had never seen before. She was magnificent. I was amazed at how confident she had become since the last time I had seen her. If indeed she was on a mission for God, she was certainly convincing. I had no idea how we were going to be received at Vaucouleurs. I imagined that when they heard our story we would be mocked and thrown out onto the streets by our ears. However, little did I realize it at the time, but from the moment we entered the walled town, Joan stepped out of the role of peasant into something we could never in our wildest dreams have imagined. From the moment we entered the doors of the governor's castle Joan was captivating. She never lacked for words, nor was she overcome by the high and mighty stature that surrounded us.

"Send the peasants away!" roared de Baudricourt when he heard who it was that was requesting an audience with him.

"You might want to see this girl, Sire," reported the gateman. "She has been talking with the guards, and they are quite impressed with her. She told them that she is on a mission for God and that she has been told by Him that you will be instrumental in bringing about the success of her calling. Which is why she has come. She has come from the southern village of Domrémy and is escorted by her cousin."

"Well, if her mission is that important, send the peasants in. This could be very amusing," chuckled the sire. "Hang around, fellow members of the court. We may be in for a bit of entertainment."

"Forgive the interruption, Sire, but I have come to tell you something very important."

"What is it, girl? Speak! We all await what it is you have come so far to tell me."

"I have come to you on the part of my Lord, Who wills that the Dauphin be made king of France as soon as possible."

"And how will this be carried out in the midst of heavy war with the English?"

"I am going to carry it out, Sire. My Lord has willed it so. I am going to escort the Dauphin from Chinon to Rheims so that he can be crowned in proper French fashion."

I could see that Sire Baudricourt and his court were shocked that such a girl could have the audacity to come into their midst with such outlandish statements and for a moment they were too stunned to respond.

"And what else does this Lord of yours say?" asked the sire, amidst a cheer of laughter and abusive remarks coming from the crowd that had gathered around them.

"He says to inform the Dauphin that he must stand steadfast against the enemy and that help is on its way."

"From you, I suppose," chuckled the sire. "And who is your Lord that you keep referring to?" he demanded.

"Why, the King of Heaven of course," Joan responded boldly. On hearing her reply, the crowed erupted into peals of laughter.

"Monsieur Laxart, would you please remove this relative of yours from my court? I am surprised you allow her to speak such barbaric remarks. Take her home immediately and punish her severely."

"Yes, Sire. Come, Joan; we must leave."

"Guards! Remove these people from my castle! We have heard enough."

However, not all those in Vaucouleurs who had heard Joan speak were ridiculing or laughing at her words as Robert de Baudricourt did. She was discouraged at first, but that was no reason for her to give up. She began to walk the streets of the town talking to anyone who would listen to her story. She regularly visited the Virgin Mary's statue and, kneeling before it, prayed that the governor would change his mind. I managed to find her lodgings in town with a friend of mine, as she did not want to return to Domrémy for fear that Jacques would punish her for her actions. I watched how the simple-hearted people of this town became moved by her faith and gradually began to believe in her cause. She made friends with a young squire, Bertrand de Poulengy, who was in the castle when she first stated her mission to the governor. He was completely moved by her story and by the bold manner in which she delivered her message in front of so many noble people. He pledged himself to her mission and told her that come time for her to leave for Chinon, he would be at her side.

"Excuse me, madam; are you the young woman that everyone here in this town is talking about? My name is Jean de Metz and I, too, have heard of your story. You seem to have everyone here sympathetic to your cause," asked a young knight who stopped her in the street one day.

"Everyone, that is, except the governor himself, and he's the one person that has the power to get me to Chinon to see the Dauphin," replied Joan. "But it doesn't matter if he agrees to help me or not. I shall go to Chinon if I have to wear my legs out doing it. You see, my Lord has willed it of me."

De Metz was entranced by her words. "If that's the case, I shall come with you. I believe in what you are doing. Joan d'Arc, you have my allegiance."

"Thank you. We shall not be alone, though. I have made

another friend: Monsieur de Poulengy, and he has offered to travel with me as well."

"You see then. You are not alone in your cause," remarked de Metz. "You have made two friends already, and both are willing to escort you all the way to Chinon, and through enemy lines at that. But I need to ask you one thing. Are you planning on making this dangerous journey dressed the way you are?"

"That aspect of my cause I had not as yet thought of," answered Joan surprisingly.

"Leave that to me. I have an idea," said de Metz.

He did not have to plan alone, because the townsfolk of Vaucouleurs began to think of Joan as something special. They began to refer to her mission as a campaign of God, that she had indeed been sent by Him to rescue France. Excitement grew as they all began to support her. Her newfound friend, de Metz, had presented her with a page boy's costume to wear on the journey, as her peasant's dress was not practical for riding. She understood and did not mind dressing in men's clothing if it meant comfort and safety for her while on the road. She began receiving riding lessons so that she could ride the horse that was given for her to make the journey as well.

The governor, seeing the support that his people were giving to this girl and that her mission was going to be carried out with or without his blessings, decided to begin publicly showing his support. The enthusiasm that she had aroused among both the residents of his town and his soldiers was nothing short of amazing. He sent a messenger to the court of Charles VII, the Dauphin, to be prepared to receive this girl that people were now calling the Maid, the girl who believed that she had been sent by God to rescue both him and the kingdom of France.

There was much excitement in the town when Joan and

her little party of escorts prepared to leave Vaucouleurs for Chinon. Everyone came to see her off. The women gathered around her in awe, eager to be near her. "Aren't you afraid to travel through enemy territory with only a few men to protect you?" one of them asked.

"They aren't the ones who are protecting me. God is my protector," replied Joan.

"You know you must travel at night to avoid the English and the Burgundian soldiers, don't you, Joan?" asked one of the men who was standing behind the women.

"Yes we do. De Metz and de Poulengy have our route worked out. We will ride by night and sleep in the forests by day. Thank you for your concern."

"You are very brave to be doing this," said another woman standing nearby.

"Madam, it is for this that I was born. Bravery has nothing to do with it."

"I see that you have gathered quite a support group since you first entered my castle, young lady," said Robert de Baudricourt, as the crowd parted to allow him through. "I almost did not recognize you in your new outfit."

"Yes, Sire. These men's clothes are far more comfortable to ride in than a cumbersome dress."

"I have come to give you my blessing and to inform you that the Dauphin is expecting you. Have you figured out what you will be saying to him?"

"The same as what I said to you, Sire. I shall inform him that his fate lies in my hands."

"Good luck, Joan. You will need it."

"Thank you, Sire."

"I have two other gifts for you," the governor went on to say. "Take this sword—you never know when you might need it—and I am sending two of my messengers along with you. Use them as you see fit."

"Thank you once again, Sire."

I embraced my cousin and bid her bon voyage. Tears ran down my cheeks as I watched her and her little party depart through the town gate out into France's harsh midwinter weather. Joan rode gallantly in front of the rest, waving to all that had come to see her off. She was followed by her two newly found friends, de Metz and de Poulengy, both gallant knights who had pledged their faith to her cause and to her safety. Close behind them rode their two servants. Then tagging on at the rear were the two newcomers to the party, the king's messengers. How brave they all looked, I thought as I watched them head out and take their dangerous path to Chinon. What would become of my little cousin? "God go with you!" I called, but they were now out of hearing. I turned and headed for home.

Chapter Five
A Perilous Journey

"The King of Heaven sends you word by me that you shall be anointed and crowned."

Jean de Metz reporting:

Chinon was far away and the 350-mile journey there was hazardous. With both the English and the Burgundian soldiers occupying the countryside, our party had to travel with caution. At night as we neared the larger towns we could hear the fanfare of the enemy soldiers entertaining themselves, so to avoid being seen we had to circle right around these larger towns. During the day, if we were lucky, we would find a deserted barn to sleep and hide our horses in, but for the most part we slept on the cold, damp ground, wrapped in our winter coats and under the cover of the thick forest. The journey was not easy. Because of the wet, wintry conditions our progress was slow and risky. The rain fell incessantly, causing the rivers to rise rapidly. Because there were English guards posted on most of the bridges, to avoid them we frequently found ourselves swimming our horses through raging currents out of sight of the bridge and the guards. Joan handled these conditions very well, and at no time did she complain or display that she was afraid.

"Wasn't it nice of the farmer to leave this old barn standing just for our use?" joked de Poulengy, as the group began to stir after a good day's sleep. "He was even kind enough to leave a couple of bales of hay for us to use as blankets."

"Let's hope there are other such barns along our route, just waiting for us to move in," I added with a chuckle.

"It's almost dark," said Joan. "We should prepare the horses to leave."

"I don't like the look of that sky," said Colet, one of the governor's messengers. "It looks like it's going to open up any moment and soak the lot of us. Wouldn't it be nice to stay in this barn for the night as well?"

"A little rain doesn't hurt anybody," added Joan, as she began loading her saddlebags.

But Colet was right. No sooner had we left our comfortable surroundings when heavy rain began to fall. In no time at all, and in spite of our winter coats, Joan and her party looked like a bunch of drowned rats. "This is turning into a real storm," I said. "Maybe we should have stayed at that barn."

"Nonsense," said Joan. "A little water is sometimes good for the soul."

Shortly after dark we came to the first major river we needed to cross. Thunder had started in deafening rolls and flashes of lightning so terrifying Colet was afraid that the trees would catch alight. We stood on the banks watching the water rising higher and higher. Although it was dark, we could still make out the shapes of trees and logs floating by before us. "If we're going to do this we had better do it now while the river is still manageable," remarked Colet.

"Maybe there's a bridge nearby," suggested Richard, the governor's second messenger.

"No, I doubt it," I replied. "Besides, we could spend all night just looking for one."

"True," said Joan, "and we don't want to waste time."

"Do you think you're up for the crossing, Joan?" asked de Poulengy.

"I'm not afraid," said Joan out loud. "I'm not afraid." But the wind and the rain whipped the words out of her mouth, as if she hadn't spoken. "Come on; let's do it." And before any of us men could stop her she had her horse headed into the waters of the raging current. We others followed. Luckily, the horses could swim well and within no time at all they had reached the other side. Unfortunately, one of the horses had snagged its leg on some floating debris and cut itself.

"We had better make camp here for the rest of the night. The horses look as if they could do with a rest," I reported as I tried to inspect the wound on my horse's leg. "Find yourself a tree and bundle yourself under it. We'll have to wait this one out."

It was a long, miserable night. However, when the first rays of light began to filter through the trees the next morning, the rain had begun to lessen. The thunderstorm had moved on and almost out of sight or hearing as we surveyed our wet surroundings. We looked back at the river that we had crossed during the night and couldn't believe our eyes. It had become a raging torrent that was about to overflow its banks. "If I had seen this during the daylight I don't think I could have ever attempted it," said Joan as she watched in disbelief. Debris of all kinds was being carried away, but what upset her most was the number of dead animals that had fallen victim to the flood. She said a prayer for those farmers who had lost them and turned away. "Let's hope that there are no more rivers like this that we have to cross."

"We had better move away from here before it claims us as well," said Richard. "How is your horse's leg?" he asked as he saw me inspecting the animal.

"It's fine. It's just a graze. Nothing to be concerned about at all."

"Good," added de Poulengy. "Then if you're all up to it, we had better mount and ride for a couple of hours. It might be a little dangerous hanging about here. Someone might come along looking for lost animals or something, sight us, and report our presence. Let's go."

For twelve days we traveled in perilous conditions in order to reach Chinon. Not once was Joan afraid of not making it. She would say to us, "Don't worry. God is leading us. My Voices tell me what we have to do in order to be safe." Her inspiration gave us motivation to carry on and to tolerate the terrible conditions we had to endure in order to reach Chinon. We had gotten used to seeing her in masculine dress, although it was hard at first. She actually looked quite striking dressed in her page's costume and bearing the sword that the governor had given her. And with her hair cut short, a would-be attacker would probably never have guessed that we included a woman in our troop. She was strong of body and made stronger by her purpose. There was a time when, riding in damp, cold clothes and with every bone in my body aching, I began to doubt our mission. I asked her, "Joan will you surely do what you say?"

In a cheerful voice she replied, "Have no fear, de Metz; what I do I do by commandment. You will see."

Her answer and the way she spoke it eliminated any doubt in my mind that we were doing the right thing, and I, too, found myself eager to arrive in Chinon to see how she would be received.

Throughout the entire journey she often mentioned how she missed hearing the mass. So it wasn't surprising that on the day we passed close to the town of Auxerre and she heard the bells at the cathedral calling people to mass, she announced that she wanted to attend.

"Joan, you can't go in there. Auxerre is a hostile town. It is full of enemy soldiers."

"I'm sure I can slip in without being noticed," said Joan.

"I can't see how," de Poulengy quickly added. "The main gates are bound to be heavily guarded."

"I'm sure I can slip by them. They're not going to suspect any trouble from a young page."

"That's true, but I'm not going to let you go in there alone. I'm coming with you," I remarked, a little angry that she should even attempt such a dangerous feat.

"I think that it would be much safer if I go alone."

"No such luck, Joan. I pledged myself to your safekeeping and I aim to do that. I shall be at your side every step of the way. De Poulengy, you stay with the others and look after the horses. We'll be back before you know it."

De Poulengy was not reassured one bit and looked very concerned when we set out on foot for the town, dressed in our disguises as merchants. He feared, as I did, that we would be recognized and ambushed. But Joan was right. We passed on by the guards in a confident manner, and they did not glance our way twice. We were not bearing arms; besides, a merchant and his page were no threat to anybody. Once inside the gates, Joan was attracted to the cathedral like a moth is to light. It was as if she needed the mass more than she needed food itself. She absorbed everything the priest had to say, and when the mass was over she stayed long after, kneeling in prayer. I was completely moved by her faith, but the longer we stayed there, the more anxious I became. When Joan was through, we exited the town in a similar manner. No questions were asked.

Richard and Colet, the governor's messengers, could not contain their excitement when they saw the Loire River looming up ahead of them. They knew that once on the other side we were in friendly territory, land faithful to Charles. "We need to find a town not too far from Chinon where we can hold up for a while and relax. From there we can send a message to the Dauphin that we have arrived and that Joan requests an audience with him. He is expecting Joan, so it should not take long for an approval."

"Sounds like a good idea," I added.

"I've been told that the little town of Fierbois, not far from Chinon, is a friendly place. Maybe we could head there and look for lodgings," said Joan.

Traveling in territory loyal to the Dauphin was a pleasure, especially for Joan. We no longer needed to avoid towns and now rode right through the middle of them. Joan frequently stopped to talk to people on the way and readily told them who she was, where she had come from, and what her purpose was. Word quickly spread in all directions that a maid from the borders of Lorraine had arrived on a mission from God and that she was being guided by Voices. A maid that was on her way to restore the king of France, fulfilling an old prophecy. She was made welcome everywhere.

No sooner had we arrived in Fierbois and found lodgings than Joan began dictating a letter to the Dauphin announcing her imminent arrival, saying that she had traveled for twelve days through enemy territory to come to his aid. "I await your invitation for an audience," it said. "Colet, is there a way I could have this delivered to the Dauphin's castle?"

"Of course, Joan. Richard and I shall take it ourselves. In that way we can ensure its safety. Would you like us to await a reply?"

"Thank you, Colet. You both have been so loyal to me. In the eyes of the Lord you shall both be richly rewarded one day."

What Joan was unaware of was the shambles that Charles's court was in. His rule was ridiculed by many, and he was looked upon as a spineless leader. His council was no better off, with deceit and bribery common practice, a place where jealousy ran rampant against any outsider who came and threatened the harmony of their deception. Charles's two closest advisers were among the worst. Georges de la Trémouille, a shameless traitor, stopped at nothing to achieve his own fallacious ends. And Regnault de Chartres, Archbishop of Rheims, although he held a high position in the Church, used it as a means to achieving wealth and power through Charles. De Chartres showed neither compassion nor sympathy toward his fellowman. These two men dominated Charles and were the true rulers of the Dauphin's domain, unfortunately, for their own selfish needs. Joan's important letter fell into the hands of these two men, who immediately branded Joan a witch. Someone who hears Voices in this manner has to be involved in witchcraft, they said, advising Charles not to see her.

Joan was never one to sit idle, so as she waited for word to come from the Dauphin, she sought out a church in town that was dedicated to Saint Catherine. It was here that Joan passed the time away listening to mass and praying beside the statue of her beloved saint. However, her impatience was growing a little thin. "Richard, why has the Dauphin not sent for me? He has had my letter for the last two days."

"I'm not sure," said de Poulengy. "Would you like to send another?"

"I shouldn't have to. He knows why I'm here. I've come to help him; why should he not want to see me?"

"He will," replied de Poulengy. "It's just a matter of time."

"Joan, are you in there?" I called as I opened the door.

"Yes, I am. Come in. We were just discussing why an invitation hasn't come from the castle."

"Well, you don't have to wait too much longer, because it has just arrived. A messenger from Chinon just delivered it moments ago."

"See, I told you, Joan," added de Poulengy. "It was just a matter of time."

"Oh, thank you, de Metz. When is it for?"

"Tomorrow. We shall leave very early in the morning."

"Great."

The following day we were met at the castle gates by a sort of welcoming committee, but they were not what Joan had quite expected.

"Why are you here?" they demanded.

"That I shall tell only to the king."

"But we are the king's counselors and it is in the name of the king that we ask these questions of you. So please answer: why are you here?"

"I have been commanded by the King of Heaven to escort Charles VII to Rheims for sacrament and his coronation. He is to be crowned the king of France in the proper manner."

"But haven't you heard? The city of Orléans is under siege. That means it's impossible to reach Rheims. So how do you expect to carry out your commands with the situation as such?"

"I need to speak to the Dauphin about that also. That is another command that I have received from the King of Heaven. To raise the siege of Orléans."

"Do you really expect us to believe you? To take you seriously?"

"Yes, I do. It has been willed in Heaven."

"Then you will need to wait a little longer while we debate these commands of yours. We shall return later."

Having the city of Orléans besieged by the enemy was a terrible setback for Charles. If the English managed to conquer the fortified city, the whole of the south of France lay open to them. If this happened, his days of power would be numbered. He remained in his castle very depressed and not wanting to think about the possibilities. He left his affairs for La Trémouille and de Chartres to take care of. However, news of the arrival of Joan d'Arc could not be suppressed. And news that she was waiting outside the gates spread throughout the castle very rapidly and soon everybody was talking about her. They all wanted to see for themselves this maid that had ridden all the way from Lorraine, insisting that she could give aid to their Dauphin. Even the courtiers' interest and curiosity had been aroused, and they insisted that Charles see this maid, this girl who claimed to be sent from God. Both La Trémouille and de Chartres's desires were overruled. Joan was sent for. However, the Dauphin did insist that before she be shown into his chamber she be questioned by the priest. If she was a witch as La Trémouille and de Chartres claimed, then surely she would back away from the holy man. However, his priest found her harmless, so he would see her.

"Noble Prince Charles," Joan said as she entered the room and knelt before him, "I am Joan d'Arc of Domrémy, but of late, people have been referring to me as Joan the Maid. I am a messenger of God here to tell you that you are the true inheritor of France, son of the king. Come to Rheims and there you shall receive the sacrament befitting a king and of course the coronation. It has been willed in Heaven."

"How am I to know that your words come from God?" asked Charles as he helped her off her knees so that he could

see her face. "And how can you perform such deeds when we are at war with the English? Have you not heard that Orléans is under siege? We have serious matters on our hands. My coronation is the least of our problems."

"I am directed by Voices," added Joan, "and they have guided me safely halfway across France, through dangerous enemy territory, to help you. Don't you think we should listen to them? My Voices come from God; rest assured of that. As for the siege of Orléans, give me soldiers and I shall go and raise that siege for you, making the way clear for you to go to Rheims. My mission is such. Please allow me to bring this about."

Charles was quite taken by this seventeen-year-old's insistence and asked himself, *Why would someone so young want to help me? The girl might be a sorceress. She had better be investigated before I take her seriously.*

The Dauphin sent Joan to Poitiers to have her examined by learned men and ecclesiastics, and for three weeks they interrogated her. They subjected her to hours of torment by asking her ridiculous questions and by having her undergo bizarre examinations to prove that she was not practicing witchcraft of any kind, nor did she have any evil intent on her mind. "Why do you say: on one hand, God wishes to deliver the people from the confines of the English, and on the other hand, He wishes you to have soldiers to drive them out? If God wills something, He doesn't need soldiers to do it," asked one of the interrogators.

"In God's name," replied Joan, "the soldiers will do battle, and God will give the victory." She was becoming a little impatient with their questions. "Listen; my Voices have given me a little over a year to achieve my mission. Could we please bring these senseless questioning sessions to an end so that I may begin my quest?"

"All in good time," they stressed. "We have to be absolutely sure of your intentions."

Eventually, the interrogation sessions were brought to an end and the results were favorable for Joan. Then, on hearing their verdict, the Dauphin accepted her story and sent for her immediately. He assigned Jean d'Aulon as her personal staff, to take care of her every need. Word spread far and wide throughout the land that the king had finally received Joan, and everyone rejoiced. Word had even reached the people in the besieged city of Orléans. It gave them the added strength and the hope that they needed to carry on with their fight. Just the thought that this mysterious Maid might soon arrive and deliver them from their plight was very good news indeed.

Joan was beginning to develop quite a following. People came from all directions to wish her well and to find out how she planned to give victory to France when no one else could. Joan tried to ignore them and concentrated her efforts on the Dauphin alone. He needed persuading that she was the person to lead an attack on Orléans, that her Voices were going to guide her.

As news spread throughout the land of Joan's mission, it fell on the ears of the young Duke of Alençon, a cousin to Charles the Dauphin. Her story so intrigued him that he rode day and night to reach his cousin's castle so that he might meet this Maid from Lorraine for himself. When he arrived he found his cousin Charles and asked if he could be introduced to Joan immediately. This was arranged, and once the formalities and introductions were taken care of, the duke sat and talked with Joan alone about her plan. He was completely taken by her story and by the confidence she displayed.

After listening to her he couldn't understand how anyone could have ever doubted her sincerity, how anyone could possibly think of her as a sorceress. Her story had touched him, and he knew he wanted to be part of it. He made a silent vow to himself that he was going to help her in any way that he could, even if his life depended upon it. He felt that she was indeed sent by God. Joan herself found his sympathetic ear pleasing. Little did she realize it at the time, but this gallant young knight who sat before her was to be so instrumental in bringing about the success of her mission. So Alençon and Jean d'Aulon joined the ranks of de Poulengy and me, the ranks to ensure the success of her mission.

Chapter Six
White Armor for Battle

"Take me to Orléans and I will show you signs of why I was chosen."

Jean d'Aulon reporting:

I had met nobody quite like her. She was driven by a desire I had seen in no one else. Time was of the utmost importance for her and she wanted things to happen instantly. I often found her on her knees and she would tell me later that she was seeking wisdom and guidance from her Voices. She often wept during these sessions as if she was hearing or seeing something that was not pleasing to her. She never ever told me what she was weeping about.

Joan had come along just when the Dauphin needed her most. He could see his territory gradually slipping away from him as the English marched on, and now that Orléans was under siege, in his mind it was just a matter of time before they would conquer it and move on to claim the south. It was a trying time for him. He needed help from anywhere he could get it. Then from out of nowhere Joan appeared, claiming that she could raise the siege of Orléans and then have him crowned the king of France at Rheims. This was indeed a turn of events for him, and he jumped at it.

"D'Aulon, is this royal decree true?"

"Yes, of course, Joan. The Dauphin has just decreed it. Word this very moment is being circulated throughout the ranks. You have been made Chief of War. Do you realize what this means, Joan?"

"No."

"It means that all captains and all other ranking officers in the Dauphin's army must follow your leadership."

"That's amazing. That means that we can leave for Orléans at once. We can begin driving those English back immediately."

"Hang on a moment, Joan. There are a lot of things to consider first, a lot of organizing to be done. For one, you can't go into battle dressed the way you are. You need a suit of armor to wear. You may be Chief of War, but that's no good with no men to command. The Dauphin's armies are scattered throughout the countryside. They need to be called together if you're planning a major attack."

"Yes, of course, d'Aulon, you're right."

"But more important, you know nothing of battle, Joan. We have to teach you a point or two about fighting: how to handle a weapon, how to control your horse. And being the Chief of War, you need to know a little about fighting strategies. No, Joan, we can't just march off to Orléans tomorrow."

"Thank you, d'Aulon; I do understand. It's just that my Voices say that I will last but a year, not much more. Therefore, I must work good and fast during this year, as there is much to do. I get a little impatient at times."

"I understand," I replied sympathetically, as I saw real concern on her face.

"I have been told that there are four things I need to accomplish in this time."

"And what are they?"

"I must raise the siege of Orléans and drive the English out of there. Free the Duke of Orléans from the hands of the English and return him to his rightful place and position. Then, finally, I must have the king crowned at Rheims. So, you see, my first task must be to raise the siege of Orléans. When this is done people will readily accept my Voices as real and from God. This is why I am anxious to begin."

"Then we must begin preparations right away."

The Dauphin was one step ahead of us. He had already sent word to his armies throughout the territories to assemble at Blois. They needed to meet their new Chief of War and practice new strategies for an assault on Orléans. There was much excitement in the land, as the word of Joan's mission had spread far and wide. They felt that God must have decided that it was time to execute the ancient prophecy. The English themselves were hearing the same news and were becoming very concerned about this girl that people were calling Joan the Maid.

"Joan, we need to leave at once for Tours," said d'Aulon one morning as he rushed into her chambers with news of the Dauphin's orders.

"Why?"

"The march is on. We need to get you started on a training program, plus the Dauphin has ordered his best armorers at Tours to construct a suit of armor for you. He told them that they must use the finest material that they have. They need you there for a fitting."

"Wonderful. I can be ready in a moment."

"I need to warn you, Joan, you have become quite the heroine. People are flocking here from afar to get a glimpse of you. You need to be prepared for that. There are villages we are going to pass through where you may be mobbed."

"Really? Do you think so?"

"Yes. And there's one other bit of news you might be interested in. A messenger has just arrived from Tours bearing the news that two of your brothers have ridden all the way from Domrémy to join you. The Dauphin has already dispatched a messenger back to Tours informing them that they are to be made a part of your personal troupe. He has commissioned his armorers there to construct suits of armor for them as well."

"That's wonderful news. I can't wait to see them. I'm eager to know how Mama and Papa are taking all this news."

Tours was a hive of activity when we arrived. Joan could not believe the reception that awaited her. People thronged about her from all directions and soldiers cheered whenever she appeared among them. The place was alive with excitement. The armor that was being shaped for her was beautiful, crafted from a type of steel that, when polished, illuminated a white, shimmering effect. When Joan rode through the crowd wearing this armor it had a profound effect on both the onlookers and on the soldiers who followed her. Wherever she turned there was love, faith, and friendship toward her by all. Even the blessings from the Church were bestowed upon her, which pleased her very much, especially after the intense questioning they had put her through in Poitiers.

"De Metz, de Poulengy, d'Aulon, come and look at my banners. Aren't they the most beautiful banners you have ever seen?"

"Yes, Joan, I'll have to say they are," I replied. "They truly are a work of art." Joan had been presented with the two banners made of white linen and silk as a sign of her devotion to her cause. One depicted the Annunciation scene and the other Christ holding up the world surrounded by angels. The background was sewn with lilies, and inscribed upon it were the words *Jesus-Maria*. "Yes, Joan, the banners are very befitting for a Maid on a mission of God—"

"Joan, there are two young men at the gate who are very anxious to see you," interrupted de Metz.

"What do they want?"

"I don't know, but they say they need to see you. I think they said their names were Jean and Pierre."

Joan jumped up and ran to the door of the chamber. "You teaser, de Metz, you know they're my brothers!" she called back to him as she ran all the way to the gate herself to let them in. "Jean! Pierre! It's me, Joan. You came all this way to join me. Come in. How is Mama? How is Papa taking the news about my mission? What did he say when you asked permission to join me?"

"How could he refuse us when his daughter ran off to war without asking his permission?" answered Pierre.

"I must say, Joan, you have certainly caused a lot of excitement in Domrémy. People can't believe the news that travelers are bringing in about you."

"We had to come to see for ourselves," Jean quickly added.

"People are hailing you as France's last hope," said Pierre. "Are they right?"

"I don't know what people are saying, but come in and I'll introduce you both to some wonderful people and I'll tell you all that has happened to me since I was thirteen years old."

"Since you were thirteen? You mean it's true, then, what we have been hearing?"

"Come and meet my friends. There will be time later for talking."

"When Durand returned to Domrémy to inform Mama and Papa as to where you had gone and that you were on a mission from God, they almost went out of their minds. They forbid Durand to mention the news to anybody else in case the scandal would ruin his position. Father figured that you had gone crazy. Mama couldn't stop crying for weeks on end, all the time praying for your recovery. They felt that you had let them down. Then news started arriving from other sources that you had gone all the way to Chinon to see the Dauphin himself and that after intense questioning he had accepted your story."

"People are now coming from all over the province to see our parents. Domrémy has never seen a day's peace since you left. Is it true," asked Pierre, "that you have been given your own horse and that special female armor is being shaped for you?"

"Yes, and armor is going to be made for the both of you as well. I'm so glad you're here. Thanks for coming. Tomorrow I begin battle lessons; you both will need to join me if you expect to fight at my side. The enemy you will be facing now won't be like the Maxey boys. None of us have had any training in warfare, so tomorrow we learn. Today is for talking anyway; come meet my personal knights."

"You have personal knights?"

"Oh, are you boys in for a shock."

The arrival of Joan's brothers was an exciting time for her. They spent the whole day and most of the night in conversation. De Metz, de Poulengy, d'Aulon, and I left them to it. We could tell that our presence was not needed.

In spite of Joan's rigorous daily schedule as she prepared for war, she took time out of her busy day to attend the cathedral. Her Voices also became more and more frequent. She learned from them that the sword that was presented to her by the governor back in Vaucouleurs was no longer suitable, that a lady of her status needed something special. They informed her that a sword befitting a maid about to raise the siege of Orléans awaited her at Fierbois and that she was to send for it. The sword was buried near the altar of Saint Catherine's Church, and it could be recognized by the five small crosses stamped on it. It was the sword that she needed to dig up and use.

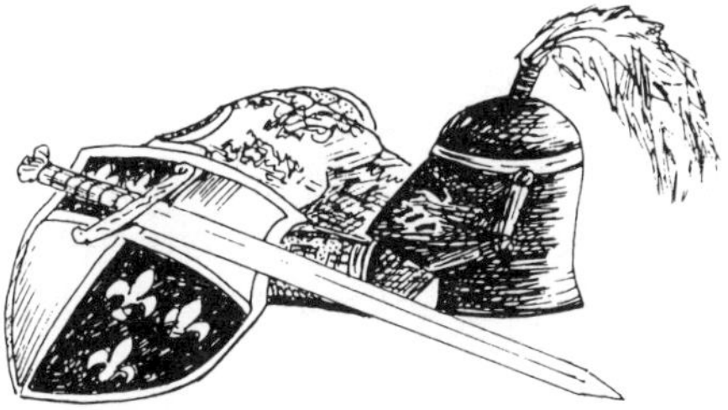

When the sword was found, cleaned, and returned to her at Tours, she was overcome with happiness. She felt very honored to receive this instrument, directed to her by word from Heaven. The sword and her banners became her proudest possessions, and she showed them off as often as she could.

With her training complete, her banners waving, her armies in waiting, and her new sword in hand, she felt she was ready to march. However, before she gave the order to march, her Voices had one more bit of news for her. She should have been upset by the knowledge, but she wasn't. It was revealed to her that she would be wounded in one of the battles ahead, at which time her blood was to flow. Not in the least bit set back, she set forth ahead of her army a very happy person. She felt that she was on the way to do the work for which she was born.

As they set out from Tours toward Blois, Joan was informed by us advisers that she was not to be concerned about the welfare of her soldiers. All details were taken care of, and there were plenty of supplies to cater to their needs. She was told that our first maneuver should be to head to Blois, pick up the rest of the soldiers who were there waiting, then head south for several days so that Orléans could be entered from friendly territory.

"Why do we want to waste our time by heading south? I thought we could head directly to Orléans and get the job over and done with quickly."

"That might not be a good idea, Maid," added one of her advisers with a concerned look on his face. "We feel that it would be safer if we approached the city from the south. Less likelihood of an attack before we join forces with our brothers in Orléans."

"Do you think this maneuver is absolutely necessary?" inquired Joan of her other advisers. She felt that this delay was yet another in a long string of unnecessary delays that had plagued them lately, but her advisers disagreed with her. "Would it not be feasible to take the more direct route with such a large army?" She knew the answer before she asked it of us, and not wanting to disagree with us on our first day out, she decided to go along with our plan. However, several days later, on our arrival at the southern side of the city, she was upset to find that the river Loire was between us and the city. Her plans of a quick attack on the English could not be. Word had gone ahead that she was coming, so those villagers owning boats came to meet us to help with the crossing. Unfortunately, there were far too many soldiers and supplies and far too few boats. She would have to send her army back to Blois to find an alternative route to Orléans.

Joan was extremely angry about the whole situation and demanded to know which of her advisers were responsible for this careless oversight. We were quick to inform her that the suggestion came from the city's hierarchy itself.

When Joan saw the city leaders crossing the river to greet them she wasted no time in questioning their motives. As she was being introduced to Count Dunois, the Count of Orléans, her displeasure was none too obvious. "Is it you that is responsible for advising us to use this southern route?" she hollered at Count Dunois, who had come to meet us on the riverbanks.

"We thought that was the best approach," he replied nervously.

"Well, you thought wrong, and for this I am having to send most of my army back to Blois to find another route. This thoughtless decision of yours has cost us a good many days and a good deal of money." Joan's advisers tried to calm her, but it was obvious that she was angry at us as well for agreeing with him. "Now I need to return to Blois with my men. Their Chief of War should lead them."

"If I may add," interrupted Count Dunois, "that might not be a good move, Maid. The people of Orléans need to see you. The whole town awaits you. If you listen carefully, you may just hear them chanting your name. They know that you are out here. If you do not make an appearance in the city, they might lose faith in you."

"He's right, Joan," I added. "We think that it better if you reside here in the city and wait for your army to return. In that way your presence will give the folk here hope and courage."

"OK, maybe you're right. Send them off with my blessing, but make sure you let them know that this was not my doing to bring them to this point only to have them sent back."

"They know, Joan."

"It's the Maid! It's the Maid!" shouted someone from the crowd as Joan d'Arc entered the southern gates of Orléans. Well-wishers had thronged the streets to get a glimpse of her and her troupe. It was a handsome sight: Joan in her shiny white armor with me and her two favorite knights, de Metz and de Poulengy, at her side. Riding close behind came her brothers Jean and Pierre. The people of Orléans were overjoyed to see the Maid and hailed her like some messiah. She had promised to come and raise their siege, and here she was. Men, women, and children pressed forward to try to touch either her or her horse as she passed by. To them she had indeed been sent by God.

Joan took advantage of the days that she had to wait for her army to return. She visited as many parts of the city that she could and of course attended mass at the church several times a day. Wherever she went, people came up to greet her and to wish her godspeed at the task she would soon undertake. Her presence inspired confidence within everyone who came into contact with her.

"D'Aulon, I need to dictate a letter to the English. They at least need to be warned that in a few days' time they are going to be attacked and that they will lose. They should be given the option of fleeing before the attack."

"Are you serious, Joan?"

"Yes. Please send for a scribe now. I feel I need to give them plenty of warning."

"They will laugh at your warning, Joan. They will think it a joke."

And laugh they did. She received a reply full of terrible insults.

"Their insults don't hurt me; they will be sorry they did not pay heed to my warning," Joan replied.

Days later the Maid's army arrived at Orléans. The huge number of men marching in such high spirits completely stunned the English garrisons. They allowed us to pass in through the city limits and into Orléans without as much as an arrow shot. No doubt messengers were immediately sent by them for reinforcements.

"Joan, wake up! I have just received word that Count Dunois has led a surprise attack on the English bastion of

Saint Loup. Wake up, Joan!" cried Pierre as he ran up the steps to her chamber. "Joan, wake up! Count Dunois has led an attack without you."

But Joan was already awake and in fact was rapidly being dressed into her armor by the madam of the house and myself. Joan's Voices had already awakened her moments before with the same news and that in order for success she needed to attack the English immediately. "Quickly, bring me my standard. Hurry! Our soldiers need me."

Within a short time Joan and her troupe were riding toward Saint Loup. "Why would Dunois do such a thing?" she asked her brother Pierre, as they rode along.

"I fear the worst, Joan!" shouted Jean d'Arc from behind as he began counting the number of wounded French soldiers returning to the city.

"Look! There's the battle!" yelled Joan as she quickly surveyed the scene before her. What she saw was very disheartening. The French were in full retreat, having suffered the worst of the battle. "Why would Dunois do such a thing without us?"

"We need to make haste, Joan. The English have the upper hand. Those French soldiers need to see you."

"Forward with God!" she called as she charged in the direction of Saint Loup, waving her standard wildly. "God is with us!" Her knights were close at her heels. Behind them were reinforcements who had gathered to follow Joan as they saw her rapidly leaving the city gates.

"It's the Maid!" came cries from both the English side and the retreating French soldiers. "It's the Maid!" The sight of the white standard and the shiny white armor bearing down upon them set up a chain reaction. Dunois's knights found regained strength and stopped their retreat, turned to face their enemy, and set forth boldly. The English became panic-stricken, dropped arms, and ran. The terrified enemy was quickly cut down by the French. It was a bloodbath; the bastion of Saint Loup was recaptured.

Surrounded by her army, Joan returned to the city. The battle had been won, and she had come through it the hero. Her soldiers were in great spirits as they returned, but she did not share their joy. It was her first battle, her first bloodshed. "Why are you not singing with us, Maid? We have much to celebrate about!" called one of her French knights.

"I know. It's just that my heart goes out to those poor English soldiers. They died without confession."

"The Lord will deliver them their just deserts," he answered back.

The victorious Maid returned to Orléans to confer with her advisers. "Now that we have one successful attack behind us, how are we to proceed with the next?" she asked of them. "We must choose the next bastion to strike and recapture." And strike she did. Joan the Maid attacked the Augustinian bastion and recaptured that in a similar fashion. With Joan at the head of the charge, her knights felt infallible. The English seeing her gallant charge waving her standard became panic-stricken and disorganized and were soon overtaken. She went on to capture her next target, the Tourelles bastion.

Joan established a ritual whereby priests would say mass to the soldiers before they headed out to battle. Those wishing to say confession could do so as well, and she urged all her men to do so. In spite of all Joan's success, there were still several elderly city leaders who were reluctant to let themselves be commanded by a peasant girl; Joan chose to ignore their feelings. God was on her side, and that was all that mattered.

The stout fortress of the Tourelles bastion proved to be a little harder to capture, mainly because of the steep embankment that had to be scaled and the two great stone towers that they used to their advantage. As the Maid was ascending a ladder to encourage her men on, the event she had been foretold occurred. "Oh no, look! The Maid has been struck!" screamed a solider on the ladder next to her.

"Help her down quickly!" shouted Jean as he rushed to the bottom of the ladder to her side. An arrow from a crossbow had struck her between the shoulder and the throat with such force that it pierced her armor and entered her body. "Keep still, Joan, while we remove your breastplate and withdraw the arrow. Be brave. It won't take long. By the looks of it you're very lucky; the point has not gone in too deep."

The enemy, seeing the Maid go down, were given new confidence. They cheered and fought on bravely.

"Take me to the nearest vineyard," said Joan to members of her personal staff. "I need to pray for strength and guidance." It was during this session that her Voices came to her once again. They spoke to her, and from them she received the stamina to carry on. Helped to her horse, she rode directly into battle once again.

The enemy, looking down, became terrified. Only moments before, the Maid had been carried from the field to die, and now she had returned to defeat them. She indeed must be a witch to work spells so powerful. They shuddered as they saw her approach. On the other hand, we French, seeing our leader reappear after being struck down, were given a new boost of strength. We fought on bravely until the English were overpowered and the bastion recaptured. Orléans had been besieged for eight months, and Joan delivered it within four days. The first part of her mission was complete. News of the deliverance spread far and wide throughout the country, and everyone celebrated. The whole of France was talking about the Maid of Orléans. She was our new hero.

Chapter Seven
Rheims and the Crown Await You

"O gentle Sire, Now the pleasure of God has been accomplished."

Duke Alençon reporting:

Those of us that remained at the castle with the Dauphin eagerly awaited the reports that messengers would bring in twice a day from Orléans. Word of the Maid's success excited everyone. Everyone, that is, except Trémouille. He was not impressed by Joan's accomplishments one bit; he had no use for war anyway, even if it was for a just cause. He preferred to resort to bribery and treachery to avoid confrontations. In actual fact, he was jealous of her. He despised her for her lowly birth and for her sudden rise to fame. It was easy for her, while he had to work hard at maintaining his position. So back at the castle while all were celebrating her achievements, he was secretly wishing her defeated.

When news arrived on the fourth day that the Maid had conquered the difficult fortress of the Tourelles bastion, a cheer could be heard throughout the entire castle. Everybody knew that it was near impossible to access the Tourelles bastion with its surrounding moat and impressive towers and this would be a true test of her skill and strength. Her victory over it was indeed worthy of jubilation. Now it would only be a matter of time before she would have the English on their heels in retreat.

And retreat they did. The next messenger came with the news that Joan had succeeded. She had raised the siege of Orléans, and the town's folk were going wild with excitement. Great celebrations were being planned in her honor.

"Alençon!" shouted the excited Dauphin.

"Yes, Sire."

"Send for every messenger that we have on hand. All of Europe must know of the Maid's victory. Send them out to announce that we have finally succeeded in defeating the English. This is the beginning of the end of their reign in France. Tell them to say that."

"Yes, Sire."

"And tell our carriage drivers to prepare to leave. We're moving camp. We're going to Tours to meet the Maid."

"Yes, Sire."

Joan was surrounded by people everywhere she went. The entire city was celebrating her conquest, offering her gifts of all kinds. But she refused them, stating that she was in need of nothing but their happiness. A great ceremony was planned to officially thank her, but she was not in need of flattery either. So in spite of the rawness of her wound, she slipped out of Orléans quietly, with a few of her personal staff accompanying her. She needed to see the Dauphin. With the first part of her mission over, she now needed to escort him to Rheims to have him crowned and she must do that at once.

She had expected to go all the way to Chinon to meet the Dauphin, but as she entered Tours she saw the flags flying that indicated the royal court was already in residence. Like Orléans, this town also was in the midst of serious celebrations. When they saw her coming, they flocked around her like sheep, eager to touch or kiss the feet of this messenger of God. Church bells rang out to announce her arrival, which caused the already-crowded streets to become an even more chaotic mass of people. Joan, not knowing how to cope with so much adoration, smiled pleasantly at them and rode on. It took all that she had to make it to Charles's residence in one piece.

Charles, also eager to greet her, ran to embrace her. "Sire, you should not be seen in this state," said Trémouille, when he saw how excited he was at seeing her. "She should come to you. You should not go running to her."

"Oh, nonsense, Trémouille, this girl is restoring my kingdom. She deserves to be honored so."

"Dauphin, I have raised the siege of Orléans," said Joan as she bowed low and embraced his legs to greet him. "The English have left."

"So I have heard, Maid. You are indeed a very brave girl."

"No. Bravery has nothing to do with it, Sire. Our victory had already been ordained in heaven. It's only the first stage in a sequence of events that will come about. You being properly crowned is the next event."

"That may be so, but now it is time to lay down arms and celebrate."

"Please come with me to Rheims," urged Joan. "Please come to Rheims and receive your crown."

"Well, that fact has to be decided upon by my advisers and counselors. They make major decisions like that for me. Now let us forget about that for a while. Come and celebrate."

"Please urge them to make their decision rapidly. Time is of the essence." Joan knew that the Dauphin had trouble making up his mind about anything and feared that the wait would be long. Trémouille was one of his head advisers, and she knew that he did not like her.

Several weeks had passed and talks after inconclusive talks were conducted, and as usual, Joan grew impatient as she saw her precious time wasting away. Finally, she took matters into her own hands and requested an audience with Charles to plead her case once again. "Noble Dauphin, please do not hold lengthy councils. I need to escort you to Rheims."

"Trémouille and the rest of my learned council feel that the time is not right for me to make such a journey. There are towns in the Loire valley, such as Jargeau and Patay, that lie between here and Rheims, that are still under English control. They feel that it is still too dangerous to set out with the situation as such. They also feel that maybe you should go out and defeat the English there first."

"So this is what your advisers think is best for you?" said Joan, a little annoyed that it had taken them so long to decide such a thing. "If this is what it takes to get you to Rheims, then so be it."

"You must leave for Orléans at once to meet with your army and advisers and begin planning a new campaign. This time I have decided to give my cousin Alençon a military command. The sooner he learns about leadership the better, but I insist he seek your advice on all matters beforehand."

"That's a wonderful idea," said Joan. She did so much enjoy my company. I seemed her favorite among her newly found loyal knightly followers.

"Charge!" shouted Joan as she signaled her army to advance. "Attack in the name of the Lord!" she continued to shout as she led her soldiers into battle. They eagerly rushed at their opponents believing that God was on their side. The sudden burst of sound was thunderous as the horses carrying their knights raced toward the Jargeau stronghold. Moments later the sound of metal clashing was just as deafening.

"Maid! Don't go too close to the front line; it's far too dangerous. It's best you stay with the second wave!" I bellowed from my horse as I watched Joan heading toward the scaling ladders being placed against the ramparts.

"Thanks for your concern, Alençon; you just worry about yourself. I'm OK," replied Joan, as she waved her standard at him.

No sooner had I issued my warning when I saw a stone go soaring through the air in her direction and make contact with the side of her head. "Quickly, someone, check on the Maid. She's down!" But my shouts were lost to the noise of the battle. However, before I had time to redirect my horse to offer assistance, Joan was on her feet shouting orders again. "That girl is truly a saint," I said to myself as I watched her pick up her standard and head toward the scaling ladders once again.

"Down with the English!" she continued to shout. "God has doomed them! They're ours already. Fight, men, like you have never fought before!"

Seeing Joan dressed all in white gave the men incredible courage. She was like their leader from Heaven, there was no stopping them, and they fought bravely. The ramparts were scaled in no time, and the English were on the run. "Jargeau will be ours soon, men. Drive every last one of them back."

It was as Joan had said. Seeing the Maid's men come scaling over the wall with such intimidating force was too much for the English, and they surrendered.

"Rest well, men, for our fight is far from over. The English are gathering an almighty force at Patay. I have been told that they are near to five thousand strong."

"Joan, maybe we should wait until we have more soldiers," I said, a little concerned at the numbers I was hearing. "We are far outnumbered. How can we beat them?"

"Young Alençon, how many times have I told you that it's not the numbers that count; it's who we have on our side. The Almighty will claim victory for us. It is He whom we should ask how we will beat them. We follow His plan."

The battle at Patay was a massacre. The English had chosen a weak defensive position, and we French were able to use this to our advantage. The cavalry did not take up its usual position to confront the English head on but split their forces in two and positioned themselves on either side of the enemy. When the alert was given to attack, they hit the English from both sides. The strategy was a success and caused them much destruction. While the English were deciding on which side to concentrate their forces, the French infantry rushed in and pounded their center field. We French fought magnificently, knowing that we had protection in Joan's faith and cause.

The English suffered a terrible defeat, losing close to two thousand troops before they surrendered or fled. It was another grand victory for Joan's army. Her successes were beginning to mount up. Joan's name was becoming a household word throughout France and much loved by all. The English, on the other hand, were beginning to hate the mere sound of it, and she became commonly known to them as the witch of Orléans, a witch who was using sorcery tactics to beat them. Word soon spread that they were willing to pay a huge reward to anyone who could capture her alive and hand her over. She needed to be put on trial for her evil deeds.

With the English garrisons fleeing from the Loire valley, many in her army wanted her to take advantage of the situation. They were advising her to continue the fight by chasing the English all the way back to Paris and then farther on to the shores of Normandy. With the English on the run and in disarray, it would be easy. But Joan had other thoughts on her mind. Now that the Loire valley was clear of English soldiers, the road to Rheims at last lay open. The Dauphin could not refuse her now.

"Maid, it is only a short two-day ride to Paris. The soldiers are in good shape and in good spirits. We could take Paris with little difficulty at all," I said eagerly, now enjoying my newfound success as a military commander.

"All in good time, Alençon. I do plan to go to Paris, but not until after the coronation; then we shall all go to Paris with the newly crowned king of France to lead us."

"But, Joan, by then the English could have brought in reinforcements. They will be much harder to fight if we wait."

"You may be right, Alençon, but for me my mission comes first. Only after the Dauphin has been crowned will I go. If I am to go anywhere at all, it must be back to Tours to collect him."

"Noble Dauphin, it is time for you to come to Rheims to collect your crown. The way is clear for us to pass."

"I don't know, Maid," he replied. The timid and cautious Charles could seldom give a direct answer. "There are still several towns along the way that have allegiances to the English," responded the Dauphin in a cowardly manner.

"Sire." Joan looked into the face of the wavering monarch. "I believe strongly that the coronation is essential to your success and to the success of France. You are a prince living in exile; crowning you in the proper fashion could unite the whole of France again."

"Yes, I agree, but is there any hurry for this?"

"Yes, Charles, there is," snapped Joan, who was beginning to lose patience with his weak, feeble, attitude. "We should leave at once!"

"Maid from Lorraine, it is obvious that you have been under a lot of stress lately. I command you to rest from the terrible hardships that you have endured. Why don't you come and meet our new soldiers? Your army keeps swelling by the day; volunteers from all over France keep arriving and are all eager to serve you. You're our hero. People want to serve you."

"Noble Dauphin, if I may say so, I cannot rest until I have escorted you to Rheims."

"If that's the case, Joan, I shall come. It seems that I am outnumbered anyway. Most of my captains agree with you that I should go to Rheims. So it shall be. We leave within the week."

Joan could not have been more cheerful. She had finally persuaded him to come, and the march was under way. From the messengers and well-wishers that kept arriving it seemed that the whole country knew that the Dauphin was on his way to be crowned. France was swept with excitement as from all over people began flocking to Rheims for the grand occasion. As we marched, those towns we came across that were once loyal to either the English or the Burgundians surrendered and swore allegiance to the soon-to-be crowned

Dauphin. As we neared Auxerre and heard the church bells ringing, she couldn't resist the temptation of taking time out to hear mass there. It was only four months earlier that she and de Metz had secretly visited the town to hear mass on their journey to Chinon. This time she would not enter the town in disguise. She would boldly walk through the gates and directly to the cathedral. And as she did, everyone who saw her stopped in their tracks to watch her pass by.

As we neared Rheims, the cathedral towers came into view and stood proud and tall. On seeing these, Joan was moved by emotion. She could not contain the tears that were beginning to streak down her face. The second stage of her mission was shortly at hand. "We are here. We are finally here," I heard her say to herself as we rode along.

"Are you OK, Joan?"

"Oh yes, Alençon. I'm just very happy."

I had never before seen her as happy as I had at this moment, and the closer we came to the city, the more ecstatic she became. I could tell that it was a great relief for her to finally deliver the Dauphin to this city. She was on the verge of achieving what she had originally set out from Domrémy to do many months ago. "What's that noise I hear?"

"It's people, Alençon. Their lookouts have spotted our arrival and have spread the word that we are here. The noise you can hear are people shouting out our welcome. Doesn't it sound wonderful?"

We had not realized just how many people had arrived in the city before us for the coronation. The streets were bustling with people. Prominent nobles intermingled with commoners, and all were pushing and shoving to get a closer look at Joan and the Dauphin. Many nobles present had recently switched their allegiance from the English and Burgundians to the Royalists. Joan had figured that this would happen. "They're so happy to see you, Joan. It must be nice to be famous."

"Joan! Joan of Lorraine. Over here! Look over here; it's us, your parents."

"Alençon, look! It's my parents. Greetings, Mama! Greetings, Papa! How are you? I am so happy to see you."

"We are happy to see you also. You look great. Look; we have brought someone with us."

"Durand Laxart! How wonderful. How are you, Durand?"

"Much better now that I have seen you. I see your wish has come true, Joan. We are all so enormously proud of you."

"It's like I told you, Durand, God is with me."

"So we have heard. You've come a long way since that cold morning we set out from Domrémy."

"I shall return soon and tell you, Mama, and Papa all about it. Where are you staying?"

"At the inn near the cathedral."

"As soon as I have delivered the Dauphin to the archbishop's palace, I shall come to the inn. I will bring Jean and Pierre with me. They are marching with the army." Joan was glad that her parents had already forgiven her for leaving Domrémy without their permission, seven months earlier.

The following morning we could hardly recognize the streets that we had passed through the day before. Carpenters had been up all night erecting grandstands and barricades to accommodate the people. The streets were now decorated with colorful banners, and gay tapestries were suspended from the windows of all buildings. It was a majestic sight befitting the occasion it was prepared for.

As Joan entered through the wide portals of the Rheims cathedral close behind the Dauphin, she felt that she was going to explode with excitement. Her Voices had asked this of her, and now it was happening. This was her doing and everyone here knew it. If someone had told her one year ago that on this day she would be standing next to the future king of France during his coronation, she would have thought them crazy. And yet here she was, doing just that. Standing close behind her were her six favorite knights: de Metz, de Poulengy, d'Aulon, her two brothers Jean and Pierre, and I. And sitting in a pew not too far away watching us all were her other three favorite people: her mother and father and dear cousin Durand. This indeed was a splendid moment for her, one she did not want to end.

She watched as the Dauphin was escorted to the high altar where the archbishop of Rheims was to perform the ceremony of consecration. He was asked to remain prostrate while special prayers were being chanted over him by the leaders of the Church. She listened as they then asked the Dauphin to recite the royal oath whereby he promised to uphold the faith, defend the church, and administer justice in ruling the kingdom of France, this kingdom that had been entrusted to him by God. She knew that before he could receive his crown he had to be anointed with the sacred oil, believed to have originally been brought by a dove from Heaven, sacred oil especially for the coronations of French kings. Once this had been done she knew that he could be draped in the royal purple cape and have the royal crown placed on his head. She waited, as did everyone in the cathedral, for the archbishop's words: "You are now king by the grace of God."

Standing not too far from Joan, I thought the walls were going to collapse around him after the crowning ceremony was over, with the trumpeters' loud fanfare and the amount of shouting and cheering that was taking place. Their Dauphin was now Charles VII, king of France. I watched Joan as she left her station and knelt before the King. I could tell that she was weeping tears of joy.

"O gentle Sire, now the pleasure of God has been accomplished."

"Rise, Joan d'Arc. You know this is all your doing?"

"No, my king, this is God's doing," replied Joan tearfully.

Later Joan was summoned once again to the king's chambers.

"Thank you for coming. I am greatly indebted to you, Joan. What is it that you want for your services? You can have anything that you desire."

"I want nothing for myself, Charles. But I would like something for my village. For years the people of Domrémy have been burdened by heavy taxes. The people there are poor and have trouble paying these taxes. I ask that they should pay no more taxes."

"Then let it be written so. That the villagers of Domrémy be exempted from paying any form of taxes* from now on. When your father returns home he shall carry a certificate from me stating that this is so."

"Thank you, my king."

"Take leave, Joan the Maid. Go and rest, because you deserve it. You have done well."

*For more than three hundred and sixty years Domrémy was allowed to exist as a tax-free village. After the Revolution this ruling was abolished.

Chapter Eight
Treachery in the Ranks

"Nothing is impossible to the power of God. Compiègne will be my limit—I am prepared."

De Poulengy reporting:

Adoration for Joan by her soldiers was tremendous. I have seen grown men throw themselves at her feet in the hope of receiving a special blessing from her. She would very politely raise them up and tell them that they would need to go to a priest to receive a blessing, that she was not qualified to give one. I often rode at her side when she was fully armored and heard every word that she muttered. She spoke as wisely as any captain, yet at heart she was just a simple girl. This is what I loved about her.

However, nothing was more touching than the devotion extended to her by the common folk. Knowing that she once came from among them made her all that more special to them. They knew she understood their plight. Whenever she was out in the streets she instantly had an audience. People fussed about her, trying to kiss her hand or touch her clothes as she passed. Parents brought little children up to her so that she might bless them, but like the requests of her soldiers, she would graciously reject their pleas.

While the people of Rheims were celebrating their recent freedom and honoring the Maid for her bravery, Joan was impatient to continue. With the English on the run and suffering from the defeat, she should attack Paris and return King Charles to his rightful place. However, when Joan suggested this, Charles was his usual slow-moving self and had other plans.

"De Poulengy, I need to see the king and urge him to bring his celebrating to an end. We still have pressing matters to take care of. The Duke of Burgundy is still in Paris with the English. We must march on them before they have time to reorganize."

"I think that's a great idea, Joan. But have you not heard? This very afternoon he heads off south to begin a tour of his kingdom."

"He can't do that! We are only a three-day march away from Paris. Within the week he could have his capital. I must speak to him at once to try to change his mind about leaving."

"He has left orders that he is not to be disturbed while

his attendants are packing for the trip. But I think he will see you."

In fact, Charles would not listen to Joan at all. He felt that he could regain Paris in other ways, so he began holding secret peace talks with the Duke of Burgundy's council. Charles figured that he was going to win the city back by diplomacy. Joan was not convinced and believed that the English and the Burgundians would not leave unless they were defeated in battle. But what neither Charles nor Joan knew of was the treachery that was going on behind their backs. Trémouille, the Archbishop of Rheims, and the Duke of Burgundy were scheming themselves. They were preparing a makeshift treaty for the ignorant Charles to sign, a treaty that would make Charles look like he was doing the right thing, thus detaining Joan from marching on Paris long enough for English reinforcements to arrive. They advised Charles to take command of his army back from Joan. This he did.

"De Poulengy, I need to do something. I fear the king's ear is being poisoned by his advisers."

"I think you are right, Joan. I also think that now he's crowned, he no longer fears capture or exile. He's allowing his counselors total right to make his decisions. They have persuaded him to travel south to Corbény, the opposite direction from Paris, and he has agreed to them."

"I have just heard that orders have been given for the entire army to ready itself to march south. And our spies in Paris have reported that English reinforcements have been arriving in the city daily. They estimate that five thousand troops have arrived in the city since the coronation."

"This is disturbing news indeed. . . . Our time for an easy capture has definitely passed," added Joan sadly. "The king is making a grave mistake."

Joan was not aware of the secret deals that were going on behind her back and that the king was just biding his time. The treaty with the Duke of Burgundy offered fifteen days' truce, promising to hand over Paris at the end of it. If Joan had known of this, she would have told him immediately that the duke was not about to hand over Paris, that he was merely playing for time. It was obvious that Paris was being strengthened to withstand attack.

When Joan found out about the secret truce, she was angry and felt betrayed. She told him that when the fifteen days were up, he would see for himself that he had been tricked. Joan was right. The truce was a means to bide time, and it worked.

Joan also knew that there were forces around Charles that opposed her every move. Hypocrisy and treachery were ripe. However, in spite of the odds that were stacked against her, Joan still wanted to attack Paris, so finally she decided to take matters into her own hands. "Alençon, I have decided to take those knights that are loyal to me and march on Paris. If you and your loyal knights joined me we could have a mighty force between us. Are you willing to come?"

"Yes, Maid. Like you, I feel that this is something we should have done a long time ago."

"Great then. We march tomorrow."

Joan and Alençon began our march with a fine body of troops, and within days we had arrived at Saint-Denis, outside the gates of Paris. When the Parisians saw us coming they were alarmed. The Maid of Orléans's reputation was enough to cause panic.

"We should really have the backing of the king," said Joan to her closest knights. "He has a lot of loyal followers in that city. If they knew that he was here with us, our presence outside these gates might be all that's needed. They might help to throw open the gates themselves without the need for an assault."

"I shall go at once to Compiègne to where the king is held up and urge him at once to join us. I think you're right. He may see the importance of his presence here and come."

"Thank you, Alençon. We shall await your return. Ride swiftly. While you're away we shall consider our best defenses and our best point of attack."

Alençon was granted an audience with King Charles, and after several pressing discussions with him, he finally agreed to come. Both he and his army marched to join the Maid. Joan, within days of having the king and his forces together, gave the cry for battle. But Paris was well protected. A deep dry trench had to be crossed first, then a high earthen rampart, and finally a moat full of water, all of which had to be overcome even before the walls of the city could be broached. "De Poulengy, arrange for bundles of wood to be brought up and used as fill!" shouted Joan, as she headed to the edge of the moat to test its depth.

"Englishmen!" shouted Joan to the defenders who were standing on the city wall looking down at her. "Surrender to King Charles now. Those who refuse will be put to death later."

"Go back to your sheep, Witch!" they shouted back. "This is no place for a peasant. Here's what we think of you and your king!" They showered Joan and her personal guards with an array of arrows.

"Maid, come back from the moat's edge. You are too close!" shouted d'Aulon. But his warning came moments too late. A shot from a crossbow bolt came flying through the air and hit her. The force was so great that it split her armor and pierced her thigh. Joan fell to the ground from the impact. Her personal guards rushed to her side and carried her back behind the earthen rampart. As her attendants were removing the arrow from her side, she managed to stagger to her feet, shouting that she was returning to the wall. D'Aulon gently persuaded her that she needed to retire for the day.

"We can't stop now. We need to carry on."

"No!" said Alençon. "You are hurt. We need to get you back to camp. The men know that you're down. They're more concerned about you than carrying on with the battle. We need to retire for the night anyway. It doesn't matter that today's assault failed. Tomorrow's another day."

Unfortunately for Joan and her captains, tomorrow's assault was not to be. During the night, the king had a change of heart and ordered the wooden bridge that Joan's men were building across the moat burned. Then in the morning he commanded Alençon and Joan to appear before him at Saint-Denis. "I have signed another truce with the Duke of Burgundy," rejoiced Charles. "He shall deliver Paris to me before Christmas. We must pack up and leave here at once. We shall leave for the Loire. My castles there await my presence."

"But, Sire, this is a big mistake. I promise you I can deliver Paris to you in a matter of days—"

"No. My decision has been made," interrupted the king.

Joan was devastated. It was now all too clear to her just how much Charles had been fooled by the Burgundians. The treachery she had suspected of going on was now complete. Then, having heard that it was Charles who had ordered the burning of her bridge, she felt desperately betrayed. Disheartened, she left his company knowing that their relationship was no longer close. The times when he followed her every word were over. He no longer listened to her or wanted her around.

"What's the matter, Joan?" asked her brothers Jean and Pierre, when they saw their sister looking so down.

"I fear my usefulness to King Charles has come to an end. Tomorrow we march away from Paris toward the Loire. My assault here has failed. My first failure. I leave tomorrow with the king, and yet my Voices are urging me to stay in Saint-Denis. What shall I do?"

"If there is not going to be an assault, then you need to leave," said Jean. "This is not the place for you to hang around."

"Joan, you have achieved so much," added Pierre. "You should not feel down." Her brother watched as she slowly walked toward her armor.

"I know that I shall never wear this again," she said. "The craftsmen at Tours never made such a fine suit before. I feel sad that it will never again see battle. Like me, its usefulness has also come to an end."

"What are you talking about, Joan?" muttered Jean. "You're talking a lot of rubbish now."

"No, Jean, I'm not. Tomorrow I shall take it to the church here and leave it there."

The two brothers stood and watched their sister leave the room. They had never seen her like this before.

As Joan had promised, the following day before leaving, she had her armor carried to the local church. Once there, she laid her armor and sword on the altar and offered them up to Saint-Denis, whose name was the war cry of France. Sadly she turned her back on them and Paris and rode away. Her will had been broken.

I had never seen Joan as impatient as she was at Loire. She was confined to the royal court by King Charles, and she hated it. Her beloved friend and close knight Alençon, who, angry at Charles for giving up his fight to rid the English, departed, headed for Normandy in pursuit of the enemy. He asked King Charles if the Maid could join him but was refused. It was a tearful farewell for her, as she knew deep down that she would never again see her favorite fighting companion, who had been at her side in almost every battle that she had fought. She missed him terribly.

Joan was made to move from castle to castle with the royal court. She was very uncomfortable, being constantly under the scrutiny of Trémouille. Finally she saw her chance to break away. The royal council was becoming alarmed at the number of towns the Burgundians were reclaiming, towns that were once loyal to Charles. Joan asked to be allowed to go and secure these towns once again. The king agreed and Joan set off with a few knights in tow. She was overjoyed and felt that she was finally back where she belonged: on the battlefield.

The end of the year was near when the new truce that Charles had signed with the Burgundians in Paris was about to end. It soon became all too clear that once again Charles had been tricked. What Joan had been telling him all along was correct. They were biding for time all along, refortifying their weak spots. Rumors of war once again were beginning to be heard throughout the land.

It was in the midst of this English comeback and while Joan was battling small pockets of English strongholds that she was visited by her heavenly counselors once again. This time they came with a warning for her that soon she would be captured, before the feast of Saint John, which was barely two months away. This was a bitter blow for her. "I still have so much to do," she told them. "If it is to be, let me die quickly, without a long captivity," she begged. They gave her no reassurance of that.

Father Pasquerel, her faithful companion since she had first received the go-ahead from Charles, tried to be comforting to her. But it was no good. She asked of him, "How can I complete my mission in such a short time?" But she knew he could not give her the answer. She then tried to rally Charles into agreeing to another attack on Paris. "Noble King, all my good work will all be for nothing if we don't act quickly. The towns to the north who had submitted to you are now being beset by the English and Burgundian raiders again. I plead with you to march on them immediately. They need your help."

"OK, I shall send them promises of aid today," he replied.

"Even Rheims is being threatened with an attack. Allow me to take men and march on them at once, before it's too late." She was thinking of Saint Catherine and Saint Margaret's words that she would be captured before Saint John's Day. To act now was of the utmost urgency.

"OK, I agree. Take all the knights that are here," said Charles. "More will come later."

"Thank you, Sire," and with that order she began to prepare. "D'Aulon, spread the word to every knight present. We march in two days."

"Yes, Maid."

"And ask my brothers Jean and Pierre if they could groom my horse for me. Also, ask Father Pasquerel if he could come and see me. There is much to be done."

While Joan was busy with her army, news arrived that the good friends of Compiègne were under siege. She made the decision to march there and provide aid. On her arrival, she discovered from de Flavy, the governor of the city, that the enemy was located in three large camps, one opposite the main gate and the other two behind the city. "I suggest we attack the middle camp opposite the main gates first. In this way we could have them defeated and have returned to the confines of the city walls before the two other camps were made aware of what had happened," suggested de Flavy.

"Sounds like a good idea to me," replied Joan.

No sooner had the main gates been thrown open when Joan gave the word to attack. Knights came pouring out of the city and headed straight toward the Burgundian camp. The attack was a surprise for them. It looked as if it would have been over in a moment had it not been for several Englishmen arriving to join one of the camps at that very moment. They saw what was happening and quickly spread the word to the two remaining camps.

"Charge, my brave knights!" yelled the Maid as she led the assault. The French soldiers from Compiègne followed close behind. The Burgundians were dropping rapidly. When success seemed only moments away, that familiar trumpet fanfare was heard coming from either side of them.

"Look! They're getting reinforcements!" screamed a voice from behind her. The Compiègnians, seeing their enemy multiplying in great numbers, began retreating toward their city.

"Fight on, my brothers! We can take them. We have God on our side." Joan and her faithful knights met the arriving troops and drove them back in a succession of charges.

"Joan, there are too many of them for us. We need to fall back behind the city wall. Hurry, Joan; they are blocking our retreat," I urged her. "We must make haste."

"Fight on, dear knights, or we are lost!"

Most of the Maid's army had retreated inside the city, leaving Joan and a few of her personal guards outside to fight alone. De Flavy, fearing that the enemy might turn on his town any moment, gave the order for the drawbridge to be raised and the city gates to be closed. The enemy was now locked outside, but so was the Maid, who with a handful of soldiers was still fighting bravely.

Now, with no escape possible, Joan and her men were

quickly surrounded. Hands from all directions reached for her in a frenzy to capture the French witch. Eventually, her cloak was grabbed and she was pulled off her horse. "How can this be?" Joan said as she fell. "Saint John's Day is still a good month away!"

De Flavy and the people of Compiègne watched from the safety of their walls as the Maid of Orléans was led away. They did nothing to help.

Chapter Nine
On Trial for Sorcery

"Wherever it may please God. I am sure neither of the time nor the place."

Father Pasquerel reporting:

I watched in horror from the walls of Compiègne as the enemy celebrated its prize capture. She was no ordinary prisoner, and they all knew it. She was captured by Jean de Luxembourg's men, which meant she now belonged to him, free to do with as he pleased. The Maid would fetch him a handsome ransom; all he needed to do was wait and see who would come up with the highest bid.

My major concern was to get word back to King Charles so that he could come to her rescue. But I should not have needed to worry about that, as news of Joan's capture flew in every direction throughout France. Within days everyone knew of it and many had begun arriving already to begin bidding for her possession. Everyone, that is, except Charles. The French Royalists did very little, if anything, to help her. Those who owed everything to her did the least. The Maid of Orléans was left to her own fate.

The battle of Compiègne may have ended, but another had begun, the battle between various factions of the Maid's enemies, each claiming the right to possess her. Joan was moved to Jean de Luxembourg's castle at Beaurevoir for safekeeping.

"Sire de Luxembourg, this witch belongs to the English," demanded Bedford, a regent for the English king, who had recently arrived from Paris to claim her. "She is a prisoner of war and should be tried as one."

"No, she does not belong to the English," interrupted Bishop Cauchon, who had come from Paris as well to represent the Church. "She was captured in my bishopric, and that means she belong to us. Because she has been accused as a witch, she must be tried in our courts to determine whether this is so."

"From what I hear, you both are accusing her of sorcery. If you joined forces and could agree on a price, you could divide the ransom between you," added de Luxembourg rather boldly.

"That might not be a bad idea," suggested Bishop Cauchon. "But whatever we decide, we need to move quickly. King Charles may have plans of his own for rescuing her."

But the bishop was wrong. Once again the indecisive Charles allowed his courtiers to make the ruling on Joan's predicament, and they had decided that as Joan had lost her usefulness, it was best to forget her. Trémouille and the Archbishop of Rheims, Charles's dishonest advisers, had much to say on the matter. The archbishop felt that Joan had become a nuisance and a troublemaker, disrupting the harmony of the royal court. Trémouille was openly pleased when he heard the news of the Maid's capture, having always resented her power over the king.

The only people who were truly grief-stricken over the maid's capture were the common folk. They banded together in many churches around the country to say mass for her. Some even marched in the streets protesting her imprisonment and the lack of concern the royal house was showing toward her capture. But these events did little to change the king's mind. He continued to ignore the situation.

Bedford and his English colleagues did want her imprisoned, but not of war; they wanted her a prisoner of the church. They meant to have her killed as soon as possible. But they wanted to make the most of her death—in a way that would discredit Charles's title as king. If they could have Joan burned as a witch, then people would see his crown as one acquired through witchcraft. It would be no title at all. "You may be right, noble de Luxembourg; the English could pay her ransom and the church could bring her to trial. Let us consult our superiors."

Joan was not treated harshly by everyone at de Luxembourg's castle. His wife, aunt, and daughter constantly visited her in her confinement. They were very kind to her and offered company during the long, tiresome days while negotiations were going on. "Joan, we are the womenfolk of Jean de Luxembourg. We have come to bring you women's clothes to change into. Surely you would now like to discard that outfit and change into something more comfortable."

"I am very glad to meet you," said Joan, "glad to see several friendly female faces after all the men that have been to peer at me. But I have to refuse your beautiful dresses. The time is not right to change my clothing yet. God will let me know when it is time to discard these clothes."

"We have been given permission to take you up onto the tower roof. Do come; you will enjoy the fresh air and the lovely scenery that can be seen from up there."

"Thank you. I would love to. Please tell me, have you heard what is to become of me? Have you heard who is offering the highest ransom?" asked Joan nervously.

"I'm afraid, Joan, as you have asked, we must be honest with you. It is the English."

Joan fell to her knees in prayer. "Dear God, let it not be true." They all knew that to be sold to the English was to be delivered to the flames. The womenfolk tried to comfort her.

"We have begged Sire de Luxembourg not to sell you to them, but he said that it was out of his hands."

Unfortunately, Joan's worst fears had come to pass. After weeks of waiting she was told that arrangements had been made. She had been sold to the English and plans were under way to have her transported to Normandy.

"Noble de Luxembourg, we have made our decision and it be wise that you accept it because there will be no better," stated Bedford.

"And what would that be?"

"We offer 10,000 gold crowns for the Maid of Orléans. She will be bought by the English and tried by the French Church. Bishop Cauchon will conduct the trial. Do you accept our offer?"

"Before I accept your offer I feel that I should wait until I hear from Charles," replied de Luxembourg.

"You won't hear from him. He has no more interest in this woman. Maybe he is finally beginning to see her as what she really is: a witch."

"Then so be it. She's yours to do as you wish."

The English felt they could count on Bishop Cauchon to do well with the job that they had expected of him and produce the desired result. And for this they would pay him handsomely. The bishop himself felt confident that he could find enough evidence of her sorcery tactics to have her condemned to death by burning. And with her death would come the downfall of Charles. The bishop eagerly looked forward to the task he was about to perform. Now it was only a matter of getting the witch to Rouen, where it was decided that the trial should take place.

It was almost two years to the day from the time Joan first set out with Durand from Domrémy, on a mission to reclaim France. The journey she was about to make now was not so daring, escorted this time by a huge party of soldiers, assigned to guard her from attempting an escape. Covered in heavy chains the way she was, there was little chance of that. The womenfolk of Beaurevoir Castle wept as they watched her go. They knew what her fate was to be.

When Joan entered the city of Rouen, people lined the streets to get a glimpse of the famous witch-girl who had so damaged the English cause. On arrival she was met by the chief jailer, the Earl of Warwick. "Joan d'Arc, you will be tried for being a heretic and a witch. You will be taken to the tower dungeon and locked there until your investigation starts. You will be chained to a block and have guards that will watch over you day and night. When we have enough evidence against you, you will be tried by the Church."

"Sire, I beg of you. If the Church is going to try me, please allow me to be placed in a Church prison so that I may be attended by nuns."

"Out of the question. Although the Church is going to try you, the English are going to pay for the trial. You are being tried as a witch; therefore, you will be treated as one. You will be deprived the luxury of a Church prison or the use of female attendants."

Joan indeed was treated cruelly. Because she was looked upon as a witch, the law required no more than that she be kept alive for her execution day. Her dungeon was dirty, bitterly cold, and damp, with windows mere slits in the wall. Because her hands and feet were heavily chained, she could not walk about, and she stayed this way day and night. She remained in these treacherous conditions for several months while Bishop Cauchon tried to gather incriminating evidence against her. He was also busy gathering men of the church to try her. Under such appalling conditions Joan would have gone quite mad if it had not been for her heavenly Voices. They were with her constantly, helping her through the long uncomfortable days and nights that she had to endure.

For several months Cauchon sent scouts out to gather evidence against her, but when they returned they had very little they could use. Cauchon was very disappointed. He would have to use Joan's reputation among the English and Burgundians for her evil doings as evidence. The trial began—sixty learned men of the Church against Joan. It was a pathetic sight.

"Rise, Joan d'Arc. The trial room awaits you," said the bailiff who came to escort her to the courthouse.

"But I need to have counsel," replied Joan. "I have no experience of a court trial. I cannot hold my own against all those men."

"You will have no counsel," responded the bailiff. "You must reply to their questions as best you can and as truthfully as you can."

"Then please, can I hear mass and have confession before the trial begins?"

"There will be no mass for you to hear. Because of the nature of your charges, you will be denied that right."

"Joan d'Arc, will you swear to tell the truth of the questions that will be asked of you?"

"I will swear willingly to my actions and to my desires, but as to the revelations from God, I will not. I have only told them to King Charles of France. They were told to me through visions and by my secret council, to reveal to nobody," Joan said to the large assemblage of learned churchmen.

Her answer created quite a stir among the men who had joined the team of judges mainly to hear what her heavenly Voices were saying. "You cannot refuse us anything!" shouted an angry member from the court bench, after hearing her response.

"May I remind you that it is you who are on trial here and you must answer any question that is asked of you," said Bishop Cauchon, who was also a little irritated that Joan should refuse to reveal her visions. "Very well, tell us how old you were when you first started receiving these Voices."

"I was thirteen when I had a Voice from God visit me in my father's garden for the first time. I was very frightened."

"Why do you think the Voice chose you?"

"I don't know, but it came with a mission for me."

"Were you given any warning that the Voice was coming?"

"Yes. Every time it came it was accompanied by a brilliant light."

"What did it sound like?" interrupted one of the judges from the bench. The entire courtroom waited with interest for her answer.

"It was a worthy Voice, and after hearing it several times, I recognized it as the Voice of an angel. Since that day this Voice has been with me guarding and advising me. I know it well."

"What did it tell you?" asked Bishop Cauchon.

"It told me that one day I would ride and fight in honor of Charles the Dauphin. That I would have him crowned the king of France, restoring him to his rightful place."

"And how did you reply to this statement?" asked Cauchon.

"That I was just a poor peasant girl with no knowledge of how to ride or to conduct myself in war."

"The next Voices you heard, do you believe them to have been those of Saint Catherine and Saint Margaret?"

"I do, and that they, too, came from God."

"Have you ever partaken in any black magic rituals?"

"No."

"Do you believe in God?"

"Yes."

"Do you have faith in God?"

"Yes."

"Who taught you about faith?"

"My mother. She taught me everything I know. She taught me the Lord's Prayer, the Hail Mary, and the Catholic creed."

"Ah, you know the Lord's Prayer then," Bishop Cauchon replied sarcastically. "Then let's hear you recite it." Cauchon knew that no witch would be able to get through the prayer without stumbling.

"I will not say the Lord's Prayer unless you hear me in confession first."

"Outrageous!" someone shouted from the benches. "She thinks we are fools."

"What have these Voices of yours told you about these court proceedings?"

"I will not answer that question. It has nothing to do with the trial. It is me you are investigating, not what my Voices say."

"Maybe you won't tell us because deep down you know that your Voices come from the Devil and not from God. Did these Voices tell you to dress like a man?"

"It was not practical to ride horses or go into battle dressed in women's wear," answered Joan.

"You are not riding a horse now!" came a shout from the bench. "Why is it then that you don't return to female dress?"

"Because my Voices have not told me to. The time is not right."

"Are you in contact with your Voices now?"

"Not right now, but when I'm alone in my cell I am. They have not forsaken me. I still receive counsel from them."

"Do your Voices speak in English?" asked the bishop.

"Why should they speak English when they are not on the English side?"

"So your saints hate the English?" asked one of the judges.

"They love what the Lord loves and hate what He hates," replied Joan.

"So you are saying that God hates the English!" shouted the same judge, as the courtroom erupted into a rowdy mob.

"I don't know. I only know that the English will be driven out of France soon."

Joan's tedious questioning continued for months. The men of the court continuously tried to trap her into revealing her visionary secrets, but whenever these questions came about she would calmly tell the court that she could not answer them. The judges often lost their tempers with her and resorted to shouting and accusing her. But Joan remained calm throughout the whole ordeal. Their questions were designed to confuse her or make her contradict herself. They tried to twist her every word into a confession of witchcraft or black magic. Nevertheless, Joan defended herself with spirit, giving calm, commonsense answers to their questions while always insisting that certain matters must remain secret. Her Voices told her so.

Finally, after endless days of being questioned and being cross-examined, it all came to an end. Bishop Cauchon suspended the trial. The proceedings were not going as planned. The Maid of Orléans was proving more difficult than he had anticipated. After months of questioning, he had not been able to prove her either a fraud or a heretic possessed by demons. Also, some of his court council were becoming sympathetic toward her story. But more important, the English were growing impatient and wanted an end to these proceedings. Cauchon dismissed his council, retaining just a handful of his obedient followers. He moved the trial to the privacy of Joan's cell and continued the questioning there. It was here, out of earshot of the masses, that the judges were able to paint her character as black as they wanted. Charges were soon written up and read to her. She was to be burned at the stake for her terrible deeds.

"If this is what's to become of me, then so be it. I rest in God's hands. All I ask of you is that you allow me to hear mass, receive the sacraments, and receive confession first."

"Joan d'Arc, you are a liar, a heretic, a blasphemer, and a witch; these privileges are not usually allowed to such criminals. But as you have been condemned to death by burning, you shall be granted your wish. You will need all the help you can get from God for the sins that you have committed," said the bishop.

Joan's days in prison were finally over. The executioner's cart came, and Joan entered it. Surrounded by soldiers, she left the prison for the Market Square, where her pyre awaited her arrival. The square thronged with people.

As the Maid bounced along in the cart, I believe she probably began to remember the past. A little more than two years before, she had been in the fields of Domrémy tending her father's cattle. She probably thought of the day her two favorite saints appeared before her; her treacherous ride to Chinon; her meeting with the Dauphin. She may have thought of her faithful captains and wondered where they all were now. How she must have missed them. She must have thought of her mother and father. The thought of them reduced her to a mess of emotions. Her life was about to come to an end, and she didn't want to die. She began to pray, fervently and devoutly, for her soul and for those who were condemning her.

"The witch is here!" cried someone from the crowd as

they saw the cart enter the marketplace.

"What does she look like?" cried another.

"She doesn't look like a witch."

"What's she doing?"

"It looks like she's praying," replied a woman onlooker.

The woman was right. Joan was praying and the prayers that she was saying were beautiful. Those of us who were around her were moved to tears. We were struck with remorse. As she prayed, she was not aware of the bundles of faggots that were being stacked around the stake. And as she was being led to the platform to receive her final sentence she continued to ask God to forgive them for what they were about to do. Bishop Cauchon repeated the charges for all to hear, then handed her over to the civil judge to complete the process.

Joan was vaguely aware of the civil judge's words to the soldiers, "Do your duty," but she felt their powerful arms wrap around her shoulders, heading her off toward the stake. The multitude of onlookers hushed to a silence.

"I beg of you, soldiers, find me a cross to hold."

"Find this woman a cross!" one shouted as they began to chain her body to the stake. A cross was hurriedly made from a couple of sticks and pushed toward her. Joan embraced it, kissed it, and pressed it to her bosom.

"Forgive them, Lord. They are too angry and confused to know what they are doing."

"Is there a final wish that you desire before the faggots are struck?" called Bishop Cauchon from the nearby platform that had been erected as viewing point of the judges.

"Yes. I would like to have a cross brought from the nearby church so that I might always have it before my eyes until my dying breath."

"Someone, go for the crucifix!" shouted Cauchon. "Let's get this over and done with."

No sooner had the crucifix appeared and been held before Joan's eyes than the faggots were struck. "Jesus, Mary, and Joseph, give me strength to endure this. Forgive them."

As the flames grew higher, many in the crowd wept uncontrollably. We heard Joan calling out the names of Michael, Saint Catherine, and Saint Margaret. Those of us that were weeping fell to our knees in remorse. "What have we done?" we cried. We continued to hear her voice long after the heat of the flames had caused us to withdraw a little. She was calling out the name of Jesus many times over. "She is asking Jesus to forgive us. What have we done?"

"We have burned a saint, that's what we have done!" shouted a voice from the crowd. "We are all lost."

Eventually, Joan's voice could be heard no more. The freedom that she had been promised had come at last. Many who had come to witness the spectacle were unable to stay. Many, including some of the judges who had tormented her for weeks on end, were overcome with sorrow as they watched the flames grow higher. They turned their faces and hurriedly rushed away. Several that looked back believed they saw the name of Jesus written in the flames.

When it was all over, the executioner ordered the soldiers to brush the unburned sticks aside and for Joan's ashes to be gathered together. They found that Joan's heart was still uncharred. As a final tribute to the witch, he ordered them to throw it, along with the ashes, into the Seine River. They wanted to hear no more about the Maid of Orléans. She was gone forever. However, they were wrong; Joan d'Arc's prevalence had only just begun.

Author's note: Joan of Arc died at the stake May 30, 1431.

Chapter Ten
Afterward

She is and deserves to be France's most popular heroine and saint.

Joan's inspiration had turned the tide of war in favor of France. She may have died, but her spirit carried on. Her mission and her prophecy all came to pass. After her death, the English hold on France weakened steadily. The Burgundians, seeing the way the war was going, eventually abandoned the English and made peace with Charles. Normandy itself, which for so long had been an English stronghold, also surrendered itself into French hands. And King Charles, in turn, finally entered Paris to return to his rightful residence.

He slowly began to regain power and prestige and began thinking and acting like a real king should. But more important, he began making decisions for himself. He soon saw the traitor his trusted counselor Trémouille really was and dismissed him with instructions never to return to the royal court. Charles also began to realize what the Maid of Orléans had been all about and that he actually had done her a grave injustice. He decided to begin proceedings to clear her name of the stain that had been put upon it when she had been sentenced to die as a heretic and a witch. He realized that the English had burned her to damage his own title to the crown, and it saddened him to think that he had been persuaded to do very little to save her.

King Charles ordered an inquiry into her life and into her trials. He sent teams of inquirers to all parts of France to interview men and women from all walks of life who had known her. A team went to Domrémy to speak to her childhood playmates, to her family, and to those who had helped her along the way. They interviewed men who had marched and fought with her as well as the men who had condemned her at her trials. All gave their testimonies** and it was from these that it was clearly shown how little Joan d'Arc deserved her fate.

After King Charles's inquiry, the pope ordered a commission to continue the inquiry and as a result declared that Joan was innocent of the charges against her. Once her innocence had been declared by the pope, great celebrations were held at Orléans, where Joan's courage had changed the course of the war.

King Charles died in 1461. Several years later his successor, Louis XI, signed a treaty with the English signifying the war was finally over. The Hundred Years War had ended, and France was united once again. The Maid of Orléans had not lived to see the victory she had earned, but she was not forgotten, this peasant girl who had believed God called her and whose faith in her Voices never wavered.

Over five hundred years after her death, Joan is still not forgotten. A movement was instituted to declare her a saint. In 1920 this came about. She was canonized by the Roman Catholic church and from then on became known by all as Saint Joan, to take her place with those whose Voices had directed her to the salvation of her people and to martyrdom. Today she lives again as the patron saint of her nation's

**Today, after five hundred years, these reports are still carefully preserved. It is from these reports that this story of Joan has been written.

armies. She is held as a divine symbol of love, devotion, and sacrifice not only in France, but throughout the entire Christian world. Those who learn of her story are quite moved by her devotion to her cause. She will live on in the hearts of many. France has declared June 24 a national holiday in her name.